KNITTING PATTERNS

SHE KNITTING PATT

OVER 30
ORIGINAL DESIGNER PATTERNS
FOR ALL YEAR ROUND

ERNS

Ebury Press

Published in Great Britain by
Ebury Press
National Magazine House
72 Broadwick Street
London W1V 2BP

ISBN 0 85223 288 8 (cased)
ISBN 0 85223 291 8 (paperback)

Printed and bound by
TONSA, San Sebastian, Spain

CONTENTS

INTRODUCTION

Hand knitting today isn't the practical, homely craft it used to be – it's a very strong element of the overall fashion scene.

I like our knitting to be an extension of the fashion pages in SHE. There are many very good leaflets produced for classic shapes in cardigans and sweaters, so I think it's our job to come up with designs which are different and exciting. Because of this the patterns SHE features aren't always straightforward to knit, but I'm sure they will inspire both beginners and more experienced handknitters alike.

When knitting or crocheting a garment, the first thing is to make sure that you understand the instructions. To the amateur, the terms used look puzzling, but this is because abbreviations are used throughout to save space. So a reader should first familiarize herself with the terms given in the 'Abbreviation Box', which precedes the main directions. For example 'K' is used for knit (plain knitting) and 'P' is used for purl. These are the two basic sts. used in the knitting patterns. In crochet it's ch. for chain, dc. for double crochet and tr. for treble. Once these abbreviations are memorized, and the method of working them known to the reader, then the instructions become clear.

In this book, the majority of garments are knitted. The prominent stitch is stocking stitch (st. st). This is only one row 'K' and the following row 'P'. After much practice at this simple stitch, the knitting needles click busily.

Knitters like to experiment, and the designs here shown are very varied – some in simple stitches and shapes, and others in Fair Isle and unusual patterns. In fact there is something for all tastes.

Running through all these designs however are two important factors: the *YARN* to be used and the *TENSION* produced from that yarn. All garments have been worked in the yarn or wool recommended and the tensions given are those the designer requires. So if proper tension isn't obtained, the garment will either be too small or too large when completed. Therefore the first thing to do is to buy the correct yarn or wool. If this is not possible, then the wool purchased must produce the accurate tension. A half-stitch in a repeat of a pattern could result in a garment 5 cm/2 ins. (inches) too large or too small. So, before beginning a design, always work out a tension sample. This sounds tedious, but it is the only way of making sure you are knitting at the same tension as the designer. When your sample corresponds to the designer's instructions, you can then proceed happily with the rest of the pattern. If however you are getting more sts. than stated for the required square, then you should try again with a larger needle – or a smaller needle if your tension square shows less stitches. Remember however, that each needle size produces a different 'row' tension as well as a stitch tension, so you must allow for this. There's no problem

if a measurement is given, but occasionally a designer quotes rows. This too must be borne in mind.

Many readers will want to aim for the 'perfect garment'. Here are a few practical hints that should be observed:

1 To keep work clean – after the first few rows have been worked – safety-pin a tea-towel or large hankie over the cast-on edge. As the work 'grows' move the safety pins up the garment, thus ensuring clean work throughout.

2 Never join on in the middle of a row – always at the beginning. There are various methods of joining, but the easiest way is to start a new ball and the end can be sewn up or down the edge of the work. This sometimes means a length of yarn is left hanging from the previous ball, but this will be used when sewing up the garment.

The exception to the rule applies to Fair Isle motifs, which could mean that another colour may need to be introduced during the working of a row. The loose ends of the motif are neatly sewn at back of work.

3 When working stocking stitch, always k. the first and last st. of every row, unless the instructions say differently. This will give a very neat edge and will help when sewing up.

4 Be careful when casting off – especially at shoulders. Many a garment is ruined by the tightening of the stitches – and the resulting 'dragged' appearance.

5 In certain garments, such as

a dolman sleeve, a shaped front of a cardigan etc, decreases and increases happen simultaneously, so read the paragraph through before continuing. This will prevent you having to 'undo your work and begin again' – frustrating to every knitter.

6 As many of the yarns to-day are synthetics, pressing the finished garment is a very important factor in the producing of the 'perfect design'. When a pattern is worked in pure wool, it is usually safe to say 'Press work with a warm iron over a damp cloth'. But with synthetics, this rule is not followed. As only the manufacturer knows what has gone into his 'yarn', he has added on the ball band a sign indicating whether the yarn can be pressed or not. So before attempting to press a mixed yarn, just read that band again. As a guide, however, the designer says what is needed in 'To Make Up'. Mohair must *never* be pressed.

7 If the work *is* to be pressed, it first must be pinned to size. You can work out the correct width of your garment (the length is usually given) by dividing the sts. quoted before the armhole shaping by the tension stated. For instance if it is 24 sts. to 10cm (4 ins.), it is therefore 6 sts. to 2½cm (1 in.). Or if you have for example 114 sts. on your needle, then 6 into 114 goes 19 times, so the width should be 48cm (19 ins.) – a correct measurement for a 91cm (36 in.) bust.

Note all jumpers should measure approx. 5cm (2 ins.)

more than the bust size required, i.e an 86cm (34 in.) bust should measure all round, 91cm (36 ins.) and a 91cm (36 in.) bust, 97cm (38 ins.). This 5cm (2 in.) leeway is necessary. For coats and loose fitting garments the leeway is much greater. Once the size required has been ascertained, be liberal with the pinning, so that when the garment is pressed it will not stretch.

8 The sewing up is very important. Many a knitter has lost 'first prize' in a knitting competition, all due to poor finishing and the inability to sew up correctly. There is no set rule, but the best method is to 'backstitch' the seams. Hold the side, shoulder and sleeve seams together and backstitch with small stitches. This will give a very neat seam. However if the yarn is very thick, a seam would be unsightly. Then it is advisable to place seams side by side and neatly stitch from side to side using a finer yarn in a similar colour.

9 When working in Fair Isle, first try a repeat or two on a sample to see the effect of the pattern and the colours. Fair Isle is very simple to do, but it does need practice to get an even surface. Always strand wools not in use loosely at back, *never* pull, otherwise your tension will get tighter and tighter and the end result will be a very small garment – *and* one which hasn't any elasticity. Catch the stranded wool at back about every 4th stitch.

10 There are not many crochet designs in this book. It is much

easier than knitting because once you have learnt the basic sts, namely, ch, dc, tr and d. tr (double treble) the remainder are just adaptations of these sts. As only one stitch is involved, any mistake that occurs can easily be remedied. However, learners always wonder why their work gets smaller and smaller. This can happen when working 'blocks' of dc or tr. – all because the worker goes in between the sts. and forgets therefore that the end st. must be worked into also. So always count the sts. before working the row and check again on completion.

11 Neckbands in either crochet or knitting can be a problem. The art of being successful is to work *into* the foundation row and not into the loose edge. This will give a small seam on the wrong side, but will appear very neat on the right side.

12 Once you have conquered all the problems and perfected your garment, why not 'ring the changes'? Find the shape and design you like best, then work it again, but introduce another stitch (of the same tension of course). A day jumper could become an 'evening out jumper'. Be adventuresome; many variations can be worked either with stitch or shape.

So get those needles clicking – a new wardrobe is just a book away!

Jane Stevens
SHE Fashion Editor

RUFFLE BLOUSE

Materials: 14(15, 16) 25g balls Emu Angorelle. 1 25g ball Emu Angorelle in contrasting colour for embroidery. A pair of 4mm (old No 8) and 3mm (old No 11) knitting needles. 2 small buttons.
Measurements: To fit an 86(91, 96) cm – 34"(36", 38") bust.
Tension: 22 sts. measures approx 10cm (4").

Abbreviations: k., Knit; p., Purl; st. (s.), stitch(es); st.st., stocking stitch; sl., slip; psso., pass slip st. over; tog., together; tbl., through back of loop; dec., decrease; inc., increase; beg., beginning; cont., continue; alt., alternate; rep., repeat; rem., remain(ing); M1, make one by picking up loop between st. just knitted and next st., and knitting or purling it through back of loop; cm, centimetres.

Size note: Where 3 figures are given follow 1st figures for 1st size, 2nd figures for 2nd size and 3rd figures for 3rd size.
Metrication note: Apart from above no mention of inches is made in the pattern.

BACK
Using 4mm needles cast on 106(112, 118) sts. and work 2 rows in st.st. Beg. shaping:
1st row: K.1, sl.1, k.1, psso., k.31, k.3 tog. tbl., k.32(38, 44), k.3 tog., k.31, k.2 tog., k.1.
2nd-4th rows: In st.st. beg. with a p. row.
5th row: K.1, sl.1, k.1, psso., k.29, k.3 tog. tbl., k.30(36, 42), k.3 tog., k.29, k.2 tog., k.1.
6th-8th rows: In st.st. beg. with a p. row. Cont. thus, dec. on next and every 4th row, working 2 sts. less between decs. until the 17th row has been worked . . . 76(82, 88) sts. rem.
18th-26th rows: In st.st. beg. with a p. row.
27th row: K.2, M1, k.23, M1, k.1, M1, k.24(30, 36), M1, k.1, M1, k.23, M1, k.2.
28th-32nd rows: In st.st. beg. with a p. row.
33rd row: K.2, M1, k.25, M1, k.1, M1, k.26(32, 38), M1, k.1, M1, k.25, M1, k.2.
34th-38th rows: In st.st. beg. with a p. row. Cont. thus inc. on next and following 6th row working 2 more sts. at centre and each end inside edge sts. – 45th row now completed and there are 100(106, 112) sts. on needle.
Now beg. with a p. row cont. in st.st. for 41 rows, thus ending with a p. row.
Shape Armholes:
Cast off 12 sts. at beg. of next 2 rows, then dec. 1 st. each end of next and every alt. row until 66(72, 78) sts. rem. thus ending after a k. row. Cont. straight for 33 rows.
Shape Shoulders:
Cast off 6(7, 8) sts. at beg. of next 4 rows and 10(11, 12) sts. at beg. of next 2 rows.

Cast off rem. sts.
RIGHT FRONT
Using 4mm needles cast on 53(56, 59) sts. and work 2 rows in st.st.
Beg. shaping:
1st row: K.1, M1, k.15, k.3 tog., k.31(34, 37), k.2 tog., k.1.
2nd row: P. to last st., M1, p.1.
3rd row: K.1, M1, k. to end.
4th row: P. to last st., M1, p.1.
5th row: K.1, M1, k.18, k.3 tog., k.29(32, 35), k.2 tog., k.1.
6th-8th rows: As 2nd-4th rows.
9th row: K.1, M1, k.21, k.3 tog., k.27(30, 33), k.2 tog., k.1.
10th-12th rows: As 2nd-4th rows.
13th row: K.1, M1, k.24, k.3 tog., k.25(28, 31), k.2 tog., k.1 . . . 54(57, 60) sts.
14th and 15th rows: As 2nd and 3rd rows.
16th row: P.
17th row: K.27, k.3 tog., k.23(26, 29), k.2 tog., k.1. Work 4 rows in st.st. beg. with a p. row.
22nd row: P.28(31, 34), cast off 2 sts., p.19 – including st. already on right-hand needle from casting off, cast off 2 sts., p.2.
23rd row: K.2, cast on 2 sts., k.19, cast on 2 sts., k. to end. Work 3 rows in st.st. beg. with a P. row.
27th row: K.1, k.2 tog. tbl., k.24, M1, k.1, M1, k.23(26, 29), M1, k.2. Work 3 rows in st.st. beg. with a p. row.
31st row: K.1, k.2 tog. tbl., k. to end.
32nd row: P.
33rd row: K.26, M1, k.1, M1, k.25(28, 31), M1, k.2.
34th row: P.
35th row: As 31st row. Work 3 rows in st.st. beg. with a p. row.
39th row: K.1, k.2 tog. tbl., k.23, M1, k.1, M1, k.27(30, 33), M1, k.2. Work 3 rows in st.st. beg. with a p. row.
43rd row: As 31st row.
44th row: P.
45th row: K.25, M1, k.1, M1, k.29(32, 35), M1, k.2.
46th row: P.
47th row: As 31st row.
48th-50th rows: In st.st. beg. with a p. row. Rep. last 4 rows 9 times more.
87th row: As 47th row.
Shape Armhole
88th row: Cast off 12 sts., p. to end . . . 37(40, 43) sts. Now keeping continuity of front decs. on every 4th row as before, *at the same time*, dec. 1 st. at end of next row and following 4 alt. rows. Work straight at armhole edge still dec. at front edge as before until 22(25, 28) sts. rem. Work 4 rows in st.st. beg. with a p. row. 131 rows of st.st. completed from beg. of shaping at lower edge of front.
Shape Shoulder:
Cast off 6(7, 8) sts. at beg. of next and following alt. row. Cast off rem. 10(11, 12) sts.
LEFT FRONT
Using 4mm needles cast on 53(56, 59) sts. and work 2 rows in st.st.

Beg. shaping:
1st row: K.1, k.2 tog. tbl., k.31(34, 37), k.3 tog. tbl., k.15, M1, k.1.
2nd row: P.1, M1, p. to end.
3rd row: K. to last st., M1, k.1.
4th row: As 2nd row.
5th row: K.1, k.2 tog. tbl., k.29(32, 35), k.3 tog. tbl., k.18, M1. k.1.
6th-8th rows: As 2nd-4th rows. Cont. thus and work to match Right Front, reversing all shapings, omitting buttonholes, casting off armhole on 87th row and shoulder on 130th row.
SLEEVES
Using 3mm needles cast on 50 sts. for each size and work 6cm in k.1, p.1 rib. Change to 4mm needles and cont. in st.st. inc. 1 st. each end of next and every following 5th row until there are 90 sts. Cont. in st.st. until work measures 43cm or length required ending after a p. row.
Shape Top
Cast off 12 sts. at beg. of next 2 rows, then dec. 1 st. each end of next and every alt. row until 54 sts. rem, ending after a p. row. Work 16 rows in st.st., then dec. 1 st. each end of every row until 34 sts. rem.
Next row: Cast off 3 sts., k. to last 2 sts., k.2 tog.
Next row: Cast off 3 sts., p. to last 2 sts., p.2 tog. Rep. last 2 rows 3 times more. Cast off rem. sts.
FRILL
Using 4mm needles cast on 16 sts. for each size.
Next row: K.
Next row: P.12, k.4. Rep. last 2 rows twice more.
Shape thus:
1st and 2nd rows: K.2, turn and k.2.
3rd and 4th rows: K.3, turn, k.3.
5th and 6th rows: K.4, turn k.4.
7th and 8th rows: K.5, turn, p.1, k.4.
9th and 10th rows: K.6, turn, p.2, k.4. Cont. in this way working across 1 more st. on each alt. row, keeping 4 sts. in garter st. at front edge until the 25th and 26th rows have been worked which read k.14, turn, p.10, k.4.
27th and 28th rows: K.13, turn, p.9, k.4.
29th and 30th rows: K.12, turn, p.8, k.4. Cont. thus working 1 st. less each alt. row until the rows k.2, turn k.2 have been worked **
Next row: K.
Next row: P. 12, k.4. Rep. last 2 rows 3 times more ***. Now rep. from ** to *** 46 times more, then from ** to ** once more. Cast off.
TO MAKE UP
Embroider pieces with French knots before sewing up. Press frill only and embroider end pieces only (otherwise wrong sides of French knots will show around neck). Darn in all loose ends. Join shoulder seams, then sew up side seams. Sew up sleeve seams, and sew in sleeves, gathering slightly at top. Now beg. at centre back and sew on frill (first pinning in position neatly). Sew on buttons to correspond with buttonholes.

CHEVRON SWEATER

Materials: 10(10, 11, 11) balls Georges Picaud Lambswool. A pair of 3mm (Old No 11) and 3¼mm (Old No 10) knitting needles. 2 small buttons.

Measurements: To fit a 91(97, 102, 107)cm – 36"(38", 40", 42") bust.

Tension: About 13½ sts. measure 5cm (2").

Abbreviations:

k., knit; p., purl; st.(s.), stitch(es); st.st., stocking stitch; cont., continue; alt., alternate; rep., repeat; foll., following; dec., decrease; inc., increase; rem., remain(ing); tog., together; beg., beginning; patt., pattern; g.st., garter stitch; tbl., through back of loop; yrn., yarn round needle; p.u.k., pick up loop before next st. and k. or p. into back of it; ch., chain; dc., double crochet; cm, centimetres; M., main; C., contrast; D., dark colour; L., light colour.

Size note: Follow 1st figures for 1st size and respective figures in brackets for larger sizes.

Metrication note: Except for materials, measurements and tension, no mention of inches is made in pattern.

Special Note:
In these instructions the beginnings and endings of the 12 row patt. are shown in brackets – 1st bracket for 1st size, 2nd bracket for 2nd size, 3rd for 3rd size and 4th for 4th size.

BACK
Using 3mm needles cast on 109(114, 120, 125) sts. and work in k.1, p.1 rib for 6cm.

Next row: * Rib 5, inc. in next st. Rep. from * ending rib 1(0, 6,5). There are now 127(133, 139, 145) sts. Change to 3¼mm needles and patt. thus:

1st row: (Wrong side) (k.3, p.6) (k.6, p.6) (p.3, k.6, p.6) (p.6, k.6, p.6) then for all sizes (k.6, p.6) 4 times, k.6, p.1, then work in reverse from the p.1 thus: k.6, (p.6, k.6) 4 times, (k.6, p.3) (p.6, k.6) (p.6, k.6, p.3) (p.6, k.6, p.6).

2nd row: (P.2, k.6) (p.5, k.6) (k.2, p.6, k.6) (k.5, p.6, k.6) then (p.6, k.6) 4 times, p.6, k.3, p.6, (k.6, p.6) 4 times, (k.6, p.2) (k.6, p.5) (k.6, p.6, k.2) (k.6, p.6, k.5).

3rd row: (K.1, p.6) (k.4, p.6) (p.1, k.6, p.6) (p.4, k.6, p.6) then (k.6, p.6) 4 times, k.6, p.5, k.6, (p.6, k.6) 4 times, (p.6, k.1) (p.6, k.4) (p.6, k.6, p.1) (p.6, k.6, p.4).

4th row: (K.6) (p.3, k.6) (p.6, k.6) (k.3, p.6, k.6) then (p.6, k.6) 4 times, p.6, k.7 p.6, (k.6, p.6) 4 times, (k.6) (k.6, p.3) (k.6, p.6) (k.6, p.6, k.3).

5th row: (P.5) (k.2, p.6) (k.5, p.6) (p.2, k.6, p.6), then (k.6, p.6) 4 times, k.6, p.9, k.6, (p.6, k.6) 4 times, (p.5) (p.6, k.2)

(p.6, k.5) (p.6, k.6, p.2).

6th row: (K.4) (p.1, k.6) (p.4, k.6) (k.1, p.6, k.6) then (p.6, k.6) 4 times, p.6, k.11, p.6, (k.6, p.6) 4 times, (k.4) (k.6, p.1) (k.6, p.4) (k.6, p.6, k.1).

7th row: (P.3, k.6) (p.6, k.6) (k.3, p.6, k.6) (k.6, p.6, k.6) then (p.6, k.6) 4 times, p.6, k.1, p.6, (k.6, p.6) 4 times, (k.6, p.3) (k.6, p.6) (k.6, p.6, k.3) (k.6, p.6, k.6).

8th row: (K.2, p.6) (k.5, p.6) (p.2, k.6, p.6) (p.5, k.6, p.6) then (k.6, p.6) 4 times, k.6, p.3, k.6, (p.6, k.6) 4 times, (p.6, k.2) (p.6, k.5) (p.6, k.6, p.2) (p.6, k.6, p.5).

9th row: (P.1, k.6) (p.4, k.6) (k.1, p.6, k.6) (k.4, p.6, k.6) then (p.6, k.6) 4 times, p.6, k.5, p.6 (k.6, p.6) 4 times, (k.6, p.1) (k.6, p.4) (k.6, p.6, k.1) (k.6, p.6, k.4).

10th row: (P.6) (k.3, p.6) (k.6, p.6) (p.3, k.6, p.6) then (k.6, p.6) 4 times, k.6, p.7, k.6, (p.6, k.6) 4 times, (p.6) (p.6, k.3) (p.6, k.6) (p.6, k.6, p.3).

11th row: (K.5) (p.2, k.6) (p.5, k.6) (k.2, p.6, k.6) then (p.6, k.6) 4 times, p.6, k.9, p.6, (k.6, p.6) 4 times, (k.5) (k.6, p.2) (k.6, p.5) (k.6, p.6, k.2).

12th row: (P.4) (k.1, p.6) (k.4, p.6) (p.1, k.6, p.6) then (k.6, p.6) 4 times, k.6, p.11, k.6, (p.6, k.6) 4 times, (p.4) (p.6, k.1) (p.6, k.4) (p.6, k.6, p.1). These 12 rows form the patt. Cont. straight in patt. until back measures 37(38, 39, 40)cm from beg.

Shape Armholes:
Cast off 7 sts. at beg. of next 2 rows, then dec. 1 st. each end of every alt. row until 101(107, 113, 119) sts. rem. Cont. on these sts., until back measures 59(60, 61, 62)cm from beg.

Shape Shoulders:
Cast off 11(11, 12, 13) sts. at beg. of next 2 rows, 11(12, 12, 13) sts. at beg. of foll. 2 rows and 11(12, 13, 14) sts. at beg. of next 2 rows. Cast off rem. sts.

FRONT
Work as for back until front measures 37(38, 39, 40)cm from beg.

Shape Armholes And Divide For Neck:
Next row:
Cast off 7 sts., patt. 56(59, 62, 65) sts. – including st. already on right-hand needle from casting off – slip centre st. on safety pin, and leave rem. sts. on spare needle. Now dec. 1 st. at armhole edge on next 6 alt. rows then cont. straight at this edge, but at the same time as armhole dec., shape neck by dec. 1 st. on next and every foll. 3rd row until 33(35, 37, 40) sts. rem. Cont. straight until work measures as back to shoulder ending at armhole edge.

Shape Shoulder:
Cast off 11(11, 12, 13) sts. at beg. of next row, 11(12, 12, 13) sts. beg. of next armhole edge row. Work next row, then cast off rem. 11(12, 13, 14) sts. Go back to other sts., rejoin yarn, work to end, then work to match other side.

SLEEVES
Using 3mm needles cast on 62 sts. for each size and work in k.1, p.1 rib for 6cm.

Next row: Inc. in 1st st., then in every 6th st . . . 73 sts.

Change to 3¼mm needles and patt. thus:

1st row: (Wrong side) (p.6, k.6) 3 times, p.1 (k.6, p.6) 3 times.

2nd row: K.5 (p.6, k.6) twice, p.6, k.3, p.6, (k.6, p.6) twice, k.5. Cont. in patt. as set inc. 1 st. each end of 6th and every foll. 8th row until there are 91(91, 95, 95) sts., working extra sts. into patt. Cont. straight until work measures 43(44, 46, 47)cm from beg. – or length required.

Shape Top:
Cast off 7 sts. at beg. of next 2 rows, then dec. 1 st. each end of every alt. row 6 times. Now dec. 1 st. at each end of every 4th row 5 times, then 1 st. each end of every row until 41(41, 45, 45) sts. rem. Cast off working 2 sts. tog. all along cast off row.

NECKBAND
Join left shoulder. Now using 3¼mm needles and with right side of work facing, pick up and k.35(37, 39, 39) sts. along back neck edge, 76 sts. down left front, 1 st. from safety pin, and 76 sts. to right shoulder. Work in g.st. for 6 rows, dec. 1 st. each side of centre st. on every row. Cast off.

SCARF
Using 3mm needles cast on 1 st. Work 3 times into st. (3 sts.). Now work in g.st., inc. 1 st. each end of next and every alt. row until there are 11 sts. On next inc. row, work first 6 and last 6 sts. in g.st. and centre st. in st.st. Cont. inc. on alt. rows, keeping 6 sts. each end in g.st. and centre sts. in st.st. until there are 23 sts., ending after a straight row.

Next row: Inc. in 1st st., k.10, p.1, k.10, inc. in last st. (25 sts.).
Next row: K.6, p.5, k.3, p.5, k.6.
Next row: Inc. in 1st st., k.9, p.5, k.9, inc. in last st. (27 sts.).
Next row: K.6, p.4, k.7, p.4, k.6.
Next row: Inc. in 1st st., k.8, p.9, k.8, inc. in last st. (29 sts.).
Next row: K.6, p.3, k.11, p.3, k.6.
Next row: Inc. in 1st st., k.7, p.6, k.1, p.6, k.7, inc. in last st. (31 sts.).
Next row: K.6, p.2, k.6, p.3, k.6, p.2, k.6. Cont. thus working in patt. as set, keeping 6 sts. each end in g.st. and inc. every alt. row as before until there are 115 sts. Work 4 rows in g.st. across all sts., still inc. as before.
Next row: K.2, k.2 tog., yrn., k. to last 4 sts., k.2 tog., yrn., k.2. Work 2 rows in g.st. and cast off.

TO MAKE UP
Press lightly using a damp cloth. Join right shoulder. Sew in sleeves, easing any fullness to top of sleeve. Sew up side and sleeve seams matching patt. Mark position of scarf and sew buttons in place.

TIP-TOP TUNIC

Materials: 9 (10, 10) 50g balls Pingouin Mohair 70. A pair of 3mm (old No 11) and 3¾mm (old No 9) knitting needles. Circular needle 3mm (old No 11).

Measurements: To fit a 86 (91, 96)cm – 34″ (36″, 38″) bust. Length from division of collar to lower edge, 90cm (35½″). Sleeve seam, 45cm (18″) – adjustable.

Tension: Approximately 23 sts. and 30 rows measure 10cm (4″) using 3¾mm needles.

Abbreviations: k., knit; p., purl; st.(s.), stitch(es); st.st., stocking stitch; dec., decrease; inc., increase; foll., following; beg., beginning; cont., continue; rem., remain(ing); cm, centimetres; tog., together; alt., alternate.

Size note: Where three figures are given follow 1st figures for 1st size, 2nd figures for 2nd size and 3rd figures for 3rd size.

Metrication Note: Except for measurements above, no mention of inches is made in pattern.

BACK

Using 3¾ needles cast on 112 (118, 124) sts. and work in k.1, p.1 rib for 10 rows, decreasing 4 sts. evenly across last row. 108 (114, 120) sts. Change to st.st. and beg. with a k. row cont. until back measures 25cm, ending after a p. row. Now dec. 1 st. at each end of next and every 16th row foll. until 98 (104, 110) sts. rem. Cont. straight until Back measures 72cm ending after a p. row.

Shape Armholes:
Cast off 3 (4, 5) sts. at beg. of next 2 rows, and 2 sts. at beg. of next 2 rows. Now dec. 1 st. at beg. of every row until 70 (74, 78) sts. rem. Leave sts. on spare needle.

FRONT

Work as Back to armhole.

Shape Armholes: Cast off 3 (4, 5) sts. at beg. of next 2 rows and 2 sts. at beg. of next 2 rows. Now dec. 1 st. at beg. of every row until 80 (84, 88) sts. rem.

Divide for Neck:
Next row: k.2 tog. k.57 (61, 65) sts., slip last 38 (42, 46) sts. on a long thread, k. to end. Work each side separately.
Next and every alt. row: p.2 tog., p. to end.
2nd row: k.6, slip these sts. on to thread, k. to end.
4th row: k.5, slip these sts. on to thread, k. to end.
6th row: As 4th row.
7th row: p.2 tog. and fasten off. Rejoin yarn to other sts.
Next row: p.6, slip sts. on to thread, p. to end.
Next row: k.2 tog., k. to end.
Now work to match other side.

SLEEVES

Using 3mm needles, cast on 52 (54, 56) sts. and work in k.1, p.1 rib for 9cm.
Next row: Rib 2 (3, 4) * rib 2, work twice into next st., rib 1. Rep. from * to last 2 (3, 4) sts., rib to end – 64 (66, 68) sts. Change to 3¾mm needles and beg. with a k. row, work in st.st. inc. 1 st. at each end of 11th and every foll. 12th row until there are 74 (78, 82) sts. Cont. straight until work measures 45cm or length required, ending after a p. row.

Shape Top:
Cast off 3 (4, 5) sts. at beg. of next 2 rows. Now dec. 1 st. at beg. of every row until 48 (50, 52) sts. rem. Leave sts. on spare needle.

YOKE

Mark the centre front with a coloured thread. Place all sts. on the circular needle and k. a round, dec. 4 sts. evenly across Back and Front and 2 sts. across each sleeve, and k. tog. the 1st and last st. of each of the 4 raglan seams – 16 sts. decreased in all – 220 (232, 244) sts. Work in rounds of k.1, p.1 rib for 12cm, ending at centre front, turn. Now cont. in rows of k.1, p.1 rib for a further 10cm, turning at centre front on each row. Cast off in rib.

MAKE UP

Sew raglan seams below yoke. Sew up side and sleeve seams.

Materials: 15(15, 16) 25g balls of Hayfields Aspen in Silver Birch (main colour). 1 50g ball of Hayfields Rendez-vous in Imperial for each size. A pair each of 4½mm (Old No 7) and 5½mm (Old No 5) knitting needles. 6 buttons. Medium size crochet hook.

Measurements: To fit a 87(91, 97)cm – 34″(36″, 38″) bust. Length from top of shoulder 58(59, 60)cm – 23″(23¼″, 23½″). Sleeve seam 46cm (18″).

Tension: 17 sts. and 22 rows measures 10cm (4″) using 5½mm needles.

Abbreviations: k., knit; p., purl; st.(s.), stitch(es); st.st., stocking stitch; inc., increase; dec., decrease; tog., together; alt., alternate; rep., repeat; patt., pattern; foll., following; cm, centimetres; rem., remain(ing); cont., continue; beg., beginning; ch., chain; dc., double crochet; htr., half treble; tr., treble; ml., make one by picking up loop and k. into back of loop; M., main colour; C., contrast.

Size note: Where 3 figures are given follow 1st figures for 1st size, 2nd figures for 2nd size and 3rd figures for 3rd size.

Metrication Note: Apart from above no mention of inches is made in pattern.

BACK

Using 4½mm needles and M. cast on 73(77, 81) sts. and work in k.1, p.1 rib for 4cm (beg. and ending right side rows with k.1).

Next row: Rib 6(8, 10) then (ml. – see abbreviations – rib 4) 15 times, ml., rib 7(9, 11) . . . 89(93, 97) sts. Change to 5mm needles and beg. with a k. row work in st.st. until Back measures 25cm ending after a wrong side row.

Shape Armholes: Cast off 5 sts. at beg. of next 2 rows, then dec. 1 st. at each end of every row until 55(57, 59) sts. rem. Work straight until Back measures 45(46, 47)cm ending after a p. row.

Shape Shoulders: Cast off 8 sts. at beg. of next 4 rows. Leave rem. 23(25, 27) sts. on spare needle.

LEFT FRONT

Using 4½mm needles and M. cast on 37(39, 41) sts. and work in k.1, p.1 rib as for Back for 4cm.

Next row: Rib 1(2, 3), then (ml., rib 5) 7 times, ml., rib 1(2, 3) . . . 45(47, 49) sts. Change to 5½mm needles and beg. with a k. row work in st.st. until Front matches Back to beg. of armhole shaping ending after a p. row.

Shape Armhole: Cast off 5 sts. at beg. of next row then work 1 row. Now dec. 1 st. at armhole edge on every row until 28(29, 30) sts. rem. Work straight until Front measures 39(40, 41)cm ending after a p. row.

Shape Neck:

Next row: K.21 sts., turn and leave rem. 7(8, 9) sts. on safety pin.

Next row: P.2 tog., p. to end. Now dec. 1 st. at neck edge on every row until 16 sts. rem. for each size. Work straight until Front matches Back to beg. of shoulder shaping ending after a p. row.

Shape Shoulder: Cast off 8 sts. at beg.

of next row. Work 1 row, then cast off rem. 8 sts.

RIGHT FRONT

Work to match Left Front, reversing all shapings.

SLEEVES

Using 4½mm needles and M. cast on 30(32, 34) sts. and work in k.1, p.1 rib for 5cm.

Next row: Rib 1(2, 3), then (ml., rib 2) 14 times, ml., rib 1(2, 3) . . . 45(47, 49) sts. Change to 5½mm needles and beg. with a k. row, work in st.st. inc. 1 st. each end of 5th and every foll. 6th row until there are 73(75, 77) sts. Work straight until sleeve measures 43cm, ending after a p. row. Cont. in patt. thus: Join on C.

Next 2 rows: In C. k. to end.

Next 6 rows: In M. in st. st. These 8 rows form the patt.

Shape Top: Keeping continuity of patt., cast off 5 sts. at beg. of next 2 rows. Work 2 rows straight. Now dec. 1 st. at each end of next and every alt. row until 37 sts. rem. for each size. Work 1 row straight then dec. 1 st. each end of every row until 21 sts. rem.

Next row: K.1, (k.2 tog.) 10 times . . . 11 sts. Cast off. Join shoulders and side seams.

PEPLUM

Using 4½mm needles M. and with right side of work facing, pick up and k. 45(47, 49) sts. along cast on edge of Left Front, 89(93, 97) sts. across Back sts. and 45(47, 49) sts. across Right Front . . . 179(187, 195) sts.

Next row: P. to end. Change to 5½mm needles and patt. thus:

1st row: In M. k.

2nd row: In M. p. Join on C.

3rd and 4th rows: In C. k. to end.

5th–8th rows: In M. work in st.st. These 8 rows form the patt. Cont. straight until peplum measures about 13cm ending after 6 rows in M. in st. st.

Next row: (Picot cast off). In C. Cast off 2 sts., * slip st. left on right-hand needle from casting off to left-hand needle, cast on 2 sts., then cast off 4 sts. (picot formed). Rep. from * to end. Fasten off.

Left Front Border:

Using 4½mm needles and M. cast on 9

sts. and rib thus:

1st row (right side): K.2, (p.1, k.1) 3 times, k.1.

2nd row: K.1, (p.1, k.1) 4 times. Rep. these 2 rows until border, slightly stretched fits up Left Front to neck edge. Cast off. Sew in position.

Right Front Border:

Mark left front border with pins as a guide for buttonholes, 1st pin 2cm from lower edge, 2nd pin 1cm from neck edge and 4 more at equal intervals between. Now work to match other border but working buttonholes at pin positions thus. Rib 3, cast off 3, rib to end. In next row cast on 3 sts. in place of those cast off.

COLLAR

Using 4½mm needles, M. and with right side of work facing, beg. at centre of right front border and pick up and k.5 sts. across border, k. across 7(8, 9) sts. left on safety pin, pick up and k. 12 sts. up right side of neck, k. across 23(25, 27) sts. from back neck, pick up and k. 12 sts down left side of neck, k. across 7(8, 9) sts. of left front safety pin, then pick up and k. 5 sts to centre of left front border, turn . . . 71(75, 79) sts. Work in k.1, p.1 rib as for Borders until work measures 5cm ending after a wrong side row.

Shape Collar

Next row: Rib 66(70, 74) sts. turn.

Next row: (Rib 61(65, 69) sts.), turn.

Next row: Rib 56(60, 64) sts., turn.

Next row: Rib 51(55, 59) sts., turn.

Next row: Rib 46(50, 54) sts., turn.

Next row: Rib 41(45, 49) sts., turn.

Cont. in rib across all sts. until collar measures 9cm at centre back, ending after a wrong side row. Break off M., join on C. and work picot cast-off edge as for peplum. Join sleeve seams, then sew in gathering fullness at top.

Armhole Picot Edging (both alike):

Using crochet hook and C. and with right side of work facing, join yarn to armhole seam (actually on the seam at Back) and * work 4 ch. miss about 1.5cm, then 1 dc. into armhole seam. Rep. from * to armhole seam at front, turn. Now into every ch. loop work 1 dc., 1 h tr., 1 tr., 1 h tr., 1 dc. Fasten off. Sew on buttons. Press seams very lightly.

MOHAIR JACKET

BOBBLE CARDIGAN

Materials: 10(11) 50g balls of Woollybear Cotton Bouclé by Patricia Roberts in main colour. 2 balls each of the same yarn in 4 contrast colours and 1 ball in a 5th contrast colour. A pair of 3¼mm (old No 10) knitting needles. 7 buttons.

Measurements: To fit an 86(91)cm — 34"(36") bust.

Tension: 10 sts. and 15 rows to 5cm (2") over pattern.

Abbreviations: k., knit; p., purl; st(s)., stitch(es); patt., pattern; st.st., stocking stitch; dec., decrease; inc., increase; alt., alternate; beg., beginning; cont., continue; rem., remain(ing); rep., repeat; m.b., make bobble thus: with colour yarn given k. 1, p.1, k. 1 all into next st., turn, p.3, turn, k.3 together; m., main; a., first contrast; b., 2nd contrast; c., 3rd contrast; d., 4th contrast; and e., 5th contrast.

Size Note: Follow 1st figures for 1st size and figures in brackets for 2nd size.

Metrication Note: Apart from measurements above no mention of inches is made in pattern.

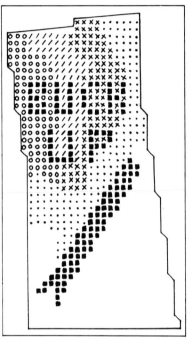

☐ = main colour   / = c
• = a   ○ = d
× = b   ■ = e

BACK

Using 3¼mm needles and m., cast on 86(91) sts. and work 12 rows in k. 1, p. 1 rib. Now beg. with a k. row work 2 rows in st. st. Now work in bobble patt. thus: This is worked entirely in st. st. except for the bobbles. Take great care not to pull colours not in use tightly across the back of the work or the garment will become puckered and lose it's elasticity.

1st row: With m. k. 3, *with a. m.b., with m. k.5. rep from *ending last rep. k3 m.

2nd, 3rd and 4th rows: With m. in st. st.

5th row: With m. k.6, *with b. m.b. with m. k.5. Rep. from *ending last rep. k.6.

6th, 7th and 8th rows: With m. in st. st.

9th to 16th rows: As 1st to 8th rows, but using c. instead of a. and d. instead of b. The last 16 rows form the bobble patt. Rep. them twice more, then work the first 14 rows again.

Shape Armholes:
Keeping continuity of patt. as set cast off 4 sts. at beg. of next 2 rows, then dec. 1 st. at

each end of next row and the 5(6) following alt. rows.... 65(69) sts. Cont. straight for 25(27) rows, then inc. 1 st. each end of next row and the 2 following 6th rows... 71(75) sts. Work 5 rows straight.

Shape Shoulders:
Cast off 10 sts. at beg. of next 2 rows and 10(11) sts. on next 2 rows. Cast off rem. 31(33) sts.

POCKET LINING

Using 3¼mm needles and m. cast on 21 sts. and beg. with a k. row work 25 rows in st. st. Leave these sts. on a spare needle.

LEFT FRONT

Using 3¼mm needles and m. cast on 33(35) sts. and work 12 rows in k.1, p.1 rib. Beg. with a k. row work 2 rows in st. st. Work in patt. thus:

1st row: With m. k.3, *with a. m.b., with m. k.5. Rep. from ending last rep. k.5 (1) m. The last row sets the position of the patt. Work to the 16th row, then work 1st-8th rows once more. Keeping continuity of patt., work across 6(7) sts., patt. next 21 sts. and leave on st. holder, work to end.

Next row: P.6(7), p. across the pocket lining sts., p. to end. Work straight for 36 rows.

Shape Armhole:
Cast off 4 sts. at beg. of next row, then dec. 1 st. at armhole edge on next 6(7) alt. rows... 23(24) sts. rem. Work 1(3) rows thus ending at armhole edge.

Shape Front:
Dec. 1 st. at end of next row and on the 3 following 6th rows... 19(20) sts. Work 5 rows straight ending at armhole edge. **Inc. 1 st. at beg. and dec. 1 st. at end of next row and the following 6th row. Work 5 rows in patt., then inc. 1 st. at beg. of next row. Work 5 rows on the 20(21) sts.

Shape Shoulder:
Cast off 10 sts. at beg. of next row and 10(11) sts. on next alt. row.

THE POCKET TOP

With right side of work facing, using m. and 3¼mm needles work in k.1, p.1. rib across the 21 sts. left on st. holder, for 6 rows. Cast off in rib.

RIGHT FRONT

Using 3¼mm needles and m. cast on 33(35) sts. and work 12 rows in k.1, p.1 rib. Beg. with a k. row work 2 rows in st. st. Now work in patt. thus:

1st row: With m. k.5(1). *with a. m.b. with m. k.5. Rep from ending last rep. with m. k.3. Work in patt. as set and complete the 16 rows of patt., then work 47 more rows straight.

Shape Armhole:
Keeping continuity of patt. cast off 4 sts. at

beg. (armhole edge) of next row, then dec. 1 st. at armhole edge on next 6(7) alt. row. 23(24) sts. rem. Work 1(3) rows thus ending at armhole edge.

Shape Front:
Dec. 1 st. at end of next row, then work back to armhole edge. Now work the BUCK UP motif thus. (This is worked entirely in st. st. so only the colour details are given. Do not weave in colours but strand yarn not in use loosely at back.)

1st row: (Wrong side) 4m., 1e., then with m. p. to end.

2nd row: Patt. as set across 17(18) sts., 1e, 4m.

3rd row: 1m., 2e., 1m., 2e., 16(17) m. The last 3 rows set position of the patt. given in the chart. Continuing to work in patt. from chart as set, work 1 row straight. Then dec. 1 st. at end of the next row and the 2 following 6th rows… 19(20) sts. Work 5 rows straight. Cont. to follow chart and work as given for left front from **to end.

SLEEVES
Using 3¼mm needles and m. cast on 61 sts. for either size and work 2 rows in st. st. Cont. in patt. as for back, inc. 1 st. each end of 11th row and every following 10th row until there are 73(75) sts. Work 15(5) rows straight.

Shape Top: Cast off 4 sts. at beg. of next 2 rows, then dec. 1 st. at each end of next row and 9(10) alt. row. Work 1 row straight, then dec. 1 st. each end of next 10 rows. Cast off 3 sts. at beg. of next 6 rows. Cast off rem. 7 sts.

FRONT BANDS AND COLLAR
(Two the same as work is reversible)
Using 3¼mm needles and m. cast on 24 sts. and work 90(94) rows in k.1, p.1 rib, then inc. 1 st. at beg. of next row and every 6th row until there are 32 sts. Work straight for 3 rows, thus ending at increased edge. Cast on 23 sts. at beg. of next row, and on the 56 sts. work 12(13) rows straight. Cast off in the rib.

CUFFS (Two the same)
Using 3¼mm needles and m. cast on 22 sts. and work 60 rows in k.1, p.1. rib. Cast off in the rib.

TO MAKE UP
Press work, except ribbed parts, on wrong side, with a warm iron over a damp cloth. Join shoulders, then sew in sleeves. Sew up sleeve and side seams. Join collar edges together, then sew collar and bands in place neatly. Sew down pocket linging and side edges of pocket tops. Sew on cuffs, then work a buttonloop at each wrist edge and sew button on other edge to fasten. Work 5 buttonloops at right front edge in position as shown in photograph, then sew on buttons at inner ribbed band edge to correspond. Press all seams.

BIG SOFTIE

CARDIGAN JACKET

Materials: Of Robin Landscape DK: 9 balls Wild Honey and 1 ball each of Squirrel, Moorland, Adriatic and Barleycorn. A pair each of 3¼mm (old No 10) and 4mm (old No 8) knitting needles. 6 buttons.

Measurements: To fit a 97-102cm (38"-40") chest, worn very loosely.

Tension: About 26 sts. and 28 rows measure 10cm (4") measured over patt.

Abbreviations: K., knit; p., purl; st.(s), stitch(es); st.st, stocking stitch; patt., pattern; beg., beginning; cm, centimetres; foll., following; alt., alternate; cont., continue; rem., remain(ing); tog., together; inc., increase; dec., decrease; rep., repeat; H, Honey, M, Moorland, S, Squirrel. A, Adriatic, B, Barleycorn.

Metrication Note: Except for above, no mention of inches is made in patterns.

The main pattern is in double moss stitch worked thus:

1st and 2nd rows: K.1, p.1 to end.
3rd and 4th rows: P.1, k.1 to end.

The colour sequence over this patt. is as follows:

1st row: In H.
2nd row: (1M, 1H) to end.
3rd, 5th and 7th rows: In H.
4th row: (1H, 1B) to end.
6th row: (1A, 1H) to end.
8th row: (1H, 1S) to end.
9th row: In H.
10th row: In H.
11th row: (1H, 1M).
12th, 14th and 16th rows: In H.
13th row: (1B, 1H) to end.
15th row: (1H, 1A) to end.
17th row: (1S, 1H) to end.
18th row: In H.

These 18 colour rows and 4 rows of double moss st. form the patt.

BACK

Using 3¼mm needles and H, cast on 134 sts. and work 17 rows in k.2, p.2 rib.

Next row: Rib 44, pick up loop before next st. and k. into it, rib 46 sts., inc. 1 as before in row, rib to end . . . 136 sts.

Change to 4mm needles and work in the 4 row patt. and colour sequence as given until Back measures 48cm from beg.

Shape Armholes:

Cast off 3 sts. at beg. of next 2 rows, then 2

sts. at beg. of next 4 rows. Now dec. 1 st. at each end of next and every alt. row until 114 sts. rem. Work straight until armhole measures 21cm, ending after a wrong side row.

Shape Shoulder and Back Neck:

Cast off 5 sts. at beg. of next 4 rows, then 4 sts. at beg. of next 4 rows (78 sts.).

Next row: Cast off 6 sts., k.26 – including st. left on right-hand needle from casting off – slip these 26 sts. on spare needle, then cast off next 14 sts., k.32. Cont. on these 32 sts. for 1st side.

Next row: Cast of 6 sts., patt. to end.
Next row: Cast off 8 sts., patt. to end.
Next row: Cast off 5 sts., patt. to end.
Next row: Cast off 8 sts., patt. to end.

Cast off rem. 5 sts. Go back to other sts., and with wrong side facing, join on wools, cast off 8 sts., patt. to end. Now work to match first side reversing shapings.

LEFT FRONT

Using 3¼mm needles and H, cast on 70 sts. and work 17 rows in k.2, p.2 rib.

Next row: Rib 22, pick up loop before next st. and k. into it, rib 26, make a st. as before in row, rib to end . . . 72 sts.

Change to 4mm needles and work in patt. until front measures as Back to beg. of armholes ending after a wrong side row.

Shape Armhole and Front:

1st row: Cast off 3 sts., patt. to last 2 sts., k.2 tog. Now cast off 3 sts. at beg. of next

3 right side rows, then 2 sts. at beg. of foll. 3 right side rows, *but at the same time,* dec. 1 st. at front edge on every 3rd row until 34 sts. rem. Cont. straight until work measures as Back to shoulder, ending after a wrong side row.

Shape Shoulder:
Cast off 5 sts. at beg. of next and foll. alt. row. Work 1 row, then cast off 4 sts. at beg. of next and foll. alt. row. Work 1 row. Cast off 6 sts. at beg. of next row and 5 sts. at beg. of next alt. row. Work 1 row, then cast off rem. 5 sts.

RIGHT FRONT
Work to match Left Front, reversing all shapings.

SLEEVES
Using 3¼mm needles and H, cast on 66 sts. and work 18 rows in k.2, p.2 rib. Change to 4mm needles and work in patt. and colour sequence as for Back, inc. 1 st. each end of 9th and every foll. 8th row until there are 94 sts. working inc. sts. into patt. Cont. straight until sleeve measures 48cm ending after same row as Back to armholes.

Shape Top.
Cast off 3 sts. at beg. of next 2 rows and 2 sts. at beg. of next 10 rows. Now dec. 1 st. each end of next and every alt. row until 40 sts. rem. Work 1 row, then cast off 2 sts. at beg. of next 2 rows and 3 sts. at beg. of next 4 rows. Cast off rem. 24 sts.

RIGHT FRONT BAND
Using 3¼mm needles and H, cast on 231 sts. and work 17 rows in k.2, p.2 rib. Cast off in rib.

LEFT FRONT BAND
Using 3¼mm needles and H, cast on 231 sts. and work 10 rows in k.2, p.2 rib.
Next row: Rib 6, * cast off 4, rib 20 – including st. already on right-hand needle from casting off, *. Rep. from * to * 4 times more, cast off 4, rib to end.
Next row: cast on 4 sts. in place of those cast off.
Rib 5 rows, then cast off in rib.

TO MAKE UP
Press work lightly avoiding the rib. Join shoulder seams. Sew in sleeves, then sew up sleeve and side seams. Place bands on wrong side of fronts with 1cm over-lapping edges and with top buttonhole just below first front neck decrease. Backstitch into place joining seam at back of neck, then stitch overlap into place on wrong side giving a neat edge. Sew on buttons.

FAIR ISLE SLIP-OVER
Materials: Of Robin Landscape DK: 4 balls in Wild Honey, 1 ball each in Squirrel, Moorland, Adriatic and Barley-corn. A pair of 3¼mm (old No 10) and 4mm (old No 8) knitting needles.
Measurements: To fit a 97-102cm (38"-40") chest.
Tension: 23 sts. and 25 rows measure 10cm (4") over Fair Isle.
BACK
Using 3¼mm needles and H, cast on 116

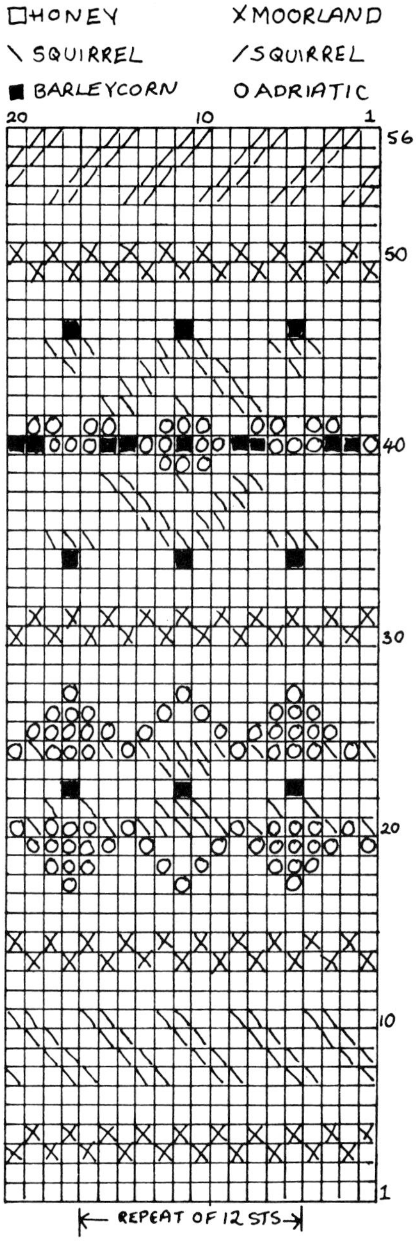

□ HONEY   X MOORLAND
\ SQUIRREL   / SQUIRREL
■ BARLEYCORN   O ADRIATIC

← REPEAT OF 12 STS →

sts. and work 20 rows in k.1, p.1 rib.
Change to 4mm needles and beg. patt., working from chart in st.st. thus:
1st and 2nd rows: In H in st.st.
3rd row: K., * 1H, 1M. Rep. from * to end.
4th row: P. * 1H, 1M. Rep. from * to end.
5th and 6th rows: In st.st. in H.
7th row: K.*1S, 2H, 1S. Rep. from * to end.
8th row: P. * 2H, 2S. Rep. from * to end.
9th row: K. * 1H, 2S, 1H. Rep. from * to end.
10th row: P. * 2S, 2H. Rep. from * to end.
11th and 12th rows: In st.st. in H.
13th row: K. * 1M, 1H. Rep. from * to end.

14th row: P. * 1M, 1H. Rep. from * to end.
15th and 16th rows: St.st. in H.
17th row: K.4 H, then rep. from 5th-16th sts. 9 times, 1A, 3H.
18th row: P. 2H, 2A then rep. from 16th-5th st., 9 times, 1A, 3H. Cont. thus and follow chart, repeating the centre 12 sts. 9 times across row, beg. and ending chart as given, and foll. sequence of patt. thus: * Rows 1-56, then rows 11-46 ** then rows 1-48 ***. At the same time when rows from * to ** have been completed.
Shape Armholes:
Cast off 4 sts. at beg. of next 2 rows, 2 sts. at beg. of next 4 rows, then dec. 1 st. each end of next k. row and foll. 8 alt. rows. Cont. straight in patt. until the complete sequence of patt. has been completed, thus ending at ***
Shape Shoulders:
Keeping continuity of patt., cast off 4 sts. at beg. of next 2 rows, 7 sts. at beg. of foll. 2 rows and 10 sts. at beg. of next 2 rows. Cast off rem. 40 sts.

FRONT
Work as for Back to armhole shaping.
Shape Armhole and Divide for Neck:
Next row: Cast off 4, patt. 54 – including st. already on right-hand needle from casting off – turn and slip rem. sts. on spare needle.
* Now cast off 2 sts. at beg. of next 2 right side rows, then dec. 1 st. at beg. of next 9 k. rows, *but at the same time as armhole decs.* are worked from *, dec. 1 st. at front edge on next 15 right side rows, then on every 3rd row at front edge until 21 sts. rem., thus ending at armhole edge. Work 2 rows straight. Front should now measure as Back to shoulder.
Shape Shoulder:
Cast off 4 sts. at beg. of next row, 2 sts. at beg. of next alt. row.
Next row: Work to end. Cast off rem. 10 sts. Go back to other sts., rejoin wools and work to match other side, reversing shapings.

NECKBAND
Join right shoulder seam. Using 3¼mm needles, H and with right side of work towards you, pick up and k.42 sts. down left side of neck, pick up st. in "V" and mark with coloured wool, pick up and k.42 sts. to shoulder and 40 sts. across back neck, turn.
Next row: P.1, k.1 rib to 2 sts. before centre st., k.2 tog., p.1, k.2 tog., rib to end. Work 9 rows more in rib, dec. 1 st. each side of centre st. Cast off in the rib, still dec. as before.

ARMBANDS
Join left shoulder and neckband seam. Using 3¼mm needles and H and with right side of work facing, pick up and k.86 sts. along armhole edge and work 10 rows in k.1,p.1 rib. Cast off in the rib.

TO MAKE UP
Press work lightly avoiding the rib. Sew up side and armband seams. Press seams.

21

PARTY PIECE

Materials: 14 (14, 15) 25g balls of Hayfield Aspen in main colour (Hazel), 2 balls in each of 2 contrast colours, Flax and Silver Birch. A pair each of 5mm (Old No 6) and 6mm (Old No 4) knitting needles. Set of four 5mm (Old No 6) needles with points each end (or short circular needle).

Measurements: To fit an 86 (91, 97)cm – 34″ (36″, 38″) bust worn loosely. Length 51 (52, 53)cm – 20″ (20½″, 21″) measured from shoulder. Sleeve seam 43 (44, 45)cm – 17″ (17½″, 18″) adjustable.

Tension: 16 sts. and 20 rows measures 10cm (4″) over st.st. using 6mm (Old No 4) knitting needles.

Abbreviations: K., knit; p., purl; st.(s.), stitch(es); st.st., stocking stitch; cont., continue; cm, centimetres; dec., decrease; foll., following; inc., increase; rem., remain(ing); rep., repeat; sl., slip; alt., alternate; beg., beginning; M, main colour; A, flax; B, silver birch.

Size Note: Where 3 figures are given follow first figures for 1st size, 2nd figures for 2nd size and 3rd figures for 3rd size.

Metrication Note: Except for above, no mention of inches is made in pattern.

BACK
Using 5mm needles and A, cast on 59 (63, 67) sts. and work thus:

1st row: K.1, (p.1, k.1) to end. Break off A, join in B.

2nd row: P.1, (k.1, p.1) to end. Cont. in rib until work measures 7cm from beg., ending with a 2nd row. Break off B, rejoin A and rib one row.

Next row: Rib 1 (3, 5) * inc. in next st., rib 2. Rep. from * to last 1 (3, 5) sts., rib to end . . . 78 (82, 86) sts. Break off A. Join in M, change to 6mm needles and beg. with a k. row cont. in st.st. until work measures 30cm from beg., ending with a p. row.

Shape Armholes:
Cast off 6 (7, 8) sts. at beg. of next 2 rows, then dec. 1 st. each end of next and every alt. row until 54 (56, 58) sts. rem, then cont. straight until armholes measure 21 (22, 23)cm ending after a p. row.

Shape Shoulders:
Cast off 8 (8, 9) sts. at beg. of next 2 rows, then 8 (9, 9) sts. at beg. of next 2 rows. Leave rem. 22 sts. on holder.

FRONT
Work as given for Back until armhole shaping is completed, then cont. straight until armholes measure 14 (15, 16)cm, ending after a p. row.

Shape Neck
Next row: K.23 (24, 25), turn and leave rem. sts. on spare needle. Now dec. 1 st. at neck edge on every alt. row until 16 (17,

18) sts. rem., then cont. straight until armhole measures as Back to shoulder ending after a p. row.

Shape Shoulder:
Cast off 8 (8, 9) sts. at beg. of next row. P.1 row, then cast off rem. 8 (9, 9) sts. Go back to sts. On spare needle, sl. first 8 sts. on to holder for neck, rejoin yarn and k. to end. Cont. to match first side.

SLEEVES
Using 5mm needles and A, cast on 31 (33, 35) sts. and work in rib as for Back, work 1 row in A, then cont. in B until work measures 7cm ending with a 2nd row. Break off B, rejoin A and rib 1 row.

Next row: Rib 1 (2, 3) * rib 2, inc. in next st., rib 1. Rep. from * to last 2 (3, 4) sts., rib to end . . . 38 (40, 42) sts. Break off A. Join in M, change to 6mm needles and cont. in st.st. inc. 1 st. each end of every 3rd row until there are 80 (82, 84) sts. – then cont. straight until sleeve measures 43 (44, 45)cm from beg. – or length required, ending after a p. row.

Shape Top
Cast off 6 (7, 8) sts. at beg. of next 2 rows, then dec. 1 st. each end of next and every alt. row until 34 sts. rem. for each size ending after a p. row.

Next row: K. 1, (k.2 tog., k.1) to end . . . 23 sts. Cast off.

COLLAR (All alike)
Join shoulder seams. Then using set of four 5mm needles beg. at centre front, sl. the first 4 sts. onto needle, then join in B and k. rem. 4 sts., pick up and k.15 sts. up right front neck, k. back neck sts., pick up and k.15 sts. down left front neck, then k. rem. 4 sts. . . . 60 sts. Cont. in rounds of k.1, p.1 rib, work 1 round in B, change to A and cont. for 3cm, ending at front edge, and working twice into last st., **turn** . . . 61 sts. Cont. in **rows** of rib, beg. and ending at centre front, working 1st and last st. in B, and rem. sts. in A, twisting the colours where they join on the wrong side of every row. Cont. for 9cm, ending with a wrong side row (wrong side of collar, which will be the right side of sweater). Break off A and work 1 row across all sts. in B. Cast off loosely in rib in B.

TO MAKE UP
First Swiss darn motifs from chart on Back, Front and Sleeves. For Back beg. on the 4th row of st.st. above welt, working 1st st. of Swiss darning in A on 4th st. (for all sizes) from left edge, working to right edge, and then on every 8th st., alternating the colour each time and working 9 (10, 10) motifs across Back. Work Front to match, but beg. 1st size with B, thus alternating each size all round Back and Front. Work Sleeves in the same way with 4 motifs in the row. Do not press. Sew up side and sleeve seams. Sew in sleeves.

SWISS DARNING
With yarn indicated and darning needle, bring needle up through the st. below the one to be covered, then pass it under the st. above the one to be covered, then pass back down through the same st. it came up through in the first place. Complete motifs.

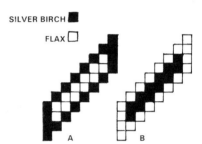

SILVER BIRCH ■

FLAX ☐

A   B

HALF-SLEEVE ROLL NECK

Materials: 10 (11, 12) 50g balls of Pingouin Natural 8 Fils. A pair of 3¼mm (Old No 10) and 4mm (Old No 8) knitting needles.
Measurements: To fit 86 (91, 97)cm – 34 (36″, 38″) bust. Length from shoulder, 58cm (23″). Sleeve seam, 15cm (6″).

Abbreviations: k., knit; p., purl; st.(s), stitch(es); cm, centimetres; st.st., stocking stitch; inc., increase; dec., decrease; tog., together; rep., repeat; M.1., make one by picking up loop before next st. and knitting into back of it; cont., continue; beg., beginning; rem., remain(ing); alt., alternate.

Size Note: Where 3 figures are given follow 1st figures for 1st size, 2nd figures for 2nd size and 3rd figures for 3rd size.
Tension: 11 sts. and 14 rows measures 5cm (2″).
Metrication Note: Except for measurements above, no reference to inches is made in pattern.

BACK
Using 3¼mm needles cast on 97 (103, 109) sts. and work in k. 1, p. 1 rib for 8cm. Change to 4mm needles and cont. in st.st. until work measures 38cm ending after a p. row.
Shape Armholes:
Cast off 3 sts. at beg. of next 2 rows then dec. 1 st. at each end of next 3 rows. Dec. 1 st. at each end of every alt. row until 79 (85, 91) sts. rem. Cont. straight until work measures 58cm, ending after a p. row.
Shape Shoulders:
Cast off 6 (7, 8) sts. at beg. of next 6 rows. Leave rem. 43 sts. on a spare needle.

FRONT
Work as for back until armhole shaping is completed, then cont. straight until there are 18 rows less than back to shoulder, thus ending after a p. row.
Shape Neck:
1st row: k. 25 (28, 31) sts. k. 2 tog., leave next 25 sts. on a spare needle for collar and rem. 27 (30, 33) sts. on st. holder.

Work 17 rows in st.st. on first set of sts., dec. 1 st. at neck edge on every right side row. There are now 18 (21, 24) sts.
Shape Shoulder:
Cast off 6 (7, 8) sts. at armhole edge on next and following 2 alt. rows. Go back to sts. on st. holder, rejoin yarn and work to match other side.

SLEEVES
Using 3¼mm needles cast on 59 sts. and work 2.5cm in k. 1, p. 1 rib. Change to 4mm needles and work thus: **1st row:** k. 2 tog., k. 27, M.1., k. 1, M.1., k. 27, k. 2 tog.
2nd row: p.
3rd row: k. 28, M.1., k. 3, M.1., k. 28.
4th row: p.
5th row: k. 2 tog., k. 26, M.1., k. 5, M.1., k. 26, k. 2 tog.
6th row: p.
7th row: k. 27, M.1., k. 7, M.1., k. 27.
8th row: p.
Cont. in this way dec. 1 st. each end of next and every following 4th row, at the same time, inc. 1 st. at each side of centre sts. on every alt. row (working 2 more sts. in centre each time) until 32 rows in all have been worked and there are 75 sts.
33rd row: k. 2 tog., k. 19, M.1., k. 33, M.1., k. 19, k. 2 tog. (75 sts.)
34th row: p.
Shape Top:
Cast off 5 sts. at beg. of next 2 rows, then dec. 1 st. at each end of next and every alt. row until 35 sts. rem.
Next row: (k. 2 tog.) 17 times, k. 1, p. next row then cast off.

COLLAR
Join right shoulder. Using 3¼mm needles pick up and k. 24 sts. down left side of front, k. across 25 sts. on spare needle, pick up and k. 25 sts. up right side of front, then finally k. across 43 back sts. (117 sts.). Work 15cm in k. 1, p. 1 rib. Cast off loosely in rib.

TO MAKE UP
Press work according to instructions on ball band. Join left shoulder and collar seam. Sew up sleeve and side seams. Sew in sleeves. Press seams.

WRAP-OVER CARDIGAN

Materials: 7 50g balls of Phildar Pegase, in grey colour (A), 2 balls of same yarn in red and 2 balls of same yarn in Lupin (B and C respectively). A 4.5mm crochet hook. A pair of 4mm (old No 8) and 3¼mm (old No 9) knitting needles. A 3¼mm (old No 9) circular knitting needle.

Measurements: To fit a 86-91cm (34"-36") bust. Measurements all round: 100cm (39½") approx. Sleeve seam, 45cm (17½").

Tension: 18 sts. and 9½ rows to 10cm (4") over patt.

Abbreviations: K., knit; p., purl; st(s)., stitch(es); ch., chain; dc., double crochet; tr., treble; sp., space; cont., continue; sl. st., slipstitch; tog., together; inc., increase; dec., decrease; foll., following; cm., centimetres; beg., beginning; patt., pattern; rep., repeat; A – grey; B – red; C – lupin.

Metrication Note: Except for measurements above, no reference to inches is made in pattern.

BACK
Using the 4.5mm hook and A, make 94 ch.

1st row: 1 tr. into 6th ch. from hook, *1 ch., miss 1 ch., 1 tr. into next ch. Rep. from *to end.

2nd row: 4 ch., 1 tr. into next tr., *1 ch., 1 tr. into next tr. Rep. from *to end, working last tr. into turning ch.… 91 sts.

3rd row: As 2nd row, joining in B on last tr. Rep. the 2nd row throughout working 3 rows each. in B, C and A until work measures 36cm from beg.

Shape Armholes:

Next row: Sl. st. over first 8 sts., patt. to last 8 sts., turn… 75 sts. Cont. in patt. until work measures 56cm from beg.

Next row: Patt. over first 25 sts., break off yarn, miss next 25 sts., rejoin yarn and patt. over remaining 25 sts. Fasten off.

LEFT FRONT
Using 4.5mm hook and A make 48 ch. and work first 2 rows as on Back… 45 sts. Cont. in patt. to match Back until work has 3 rows less than Back to armhole.

Shape Front

Next row: Patt. to last 2 sts., turn. Work 2 rows.

Shape Armhole

Next row: Sl. st. over first 2 sts., patt. to last 8 sts., turn. Cont. to dec. 2 sts. at front edge on every 3rd row 4 more times – 25 sts. remain, then cont. straight until work measures as Back to shoulder. Fasten off.

RIGHT FRONT
Work to match Left Front, reversing all shapings.

SLEEVES
Using 4.5mm hook and C, make 58 ch. and work first 2 rows as on Back… 55 sts. Cont. in patt. inc. 2 sts. (ie, 1 tr. and 1 ch.) at each end of 5th and every foll. 6th row until there are 75 sts. Cont. straight until work measures 36cm from beg. Place a marker at each end of last row then work straight for a further 5cm. Fasten off.

CUFFS
Using the 3¼mm knitting needles and A, and with right side of work facing, pick up and k. 54 sts. along foundation ch. of sleeve.

1st row: P.2, *k. 2, p. 2. Rep. from* to end.

2nd row: K. 2, *p. 2, k. 2. Rep. from* to end. Rep. these 2 rows for 4cm. Cast off loosely in rib.

FRONT BORDER
Join shoulders. Then using the circular needle and A and with right side of work facing, pick up and k. 118 sts. up right front edge, 26 sts. across back neck, 118 sts. down left front… 262 sts. on needle, turn. Work backwards and forwards in k. 2. p. 2 rib as on cuffs for 4cm. Cast off loosely in rib.

TO MAKE UP
Using yarn double, weave through the crochet pattern spaces as shown in picture, beg. at right front edge with C and working 3 rows each in C, A and B until all pieces are woven. Work sleeves the same way. Darn in all ends neatly. Sew in sleeves sewing the last 5cm of sleeve to the cast off armhole sts. Join side and sleeve seams. Now using A, work a row of dc. all round lower edge. Press seams lightly with a cool iron over a dry cloth.

FAIR ISLE TWIN SET

Materials: *For Cardigan:* 14 balls in grey, Hayfield Gossamer Mohair, 2 balls each in rust and beige of the same yarn.
For Waistcoat: 7 balls in grey Hayfield Gossamer Mohair, 3 balls in beige and 2 balls in rust of the same yarn. For both designs, a pair of 5½mm (Old No 5) and 7½mm (Old No 1) knitting needles and 6 buttons.
Measurements: To fit a 91-97cm (36"-38") bust. (Cardigan worn very loosely.)
Tension: Approx 3½ sts and 4 rows to 2½cm (1") using 7½mm needles.
Metrications Note: Except for measurements above, no mention of inches is made in pattern.

Abbreviations: K., knit; p., purl; st(s)., stitch(es); st.st., stocking stitch; rep., repeat; cont., continue; beg., beginning; tbl., through back of loop; inc., increase; cm., centimetres; grey – main colour A; B – rust, 1st contrast; C – beige, 2nd contrast; patt., pattern; rem., remaining.

THE CARDIGAN

BACK Using A and 5½mm needles cast on 60 sts. and work in twisted rib thus:
Next row: * K.1, tbl., p.1. Rep. from * to end. Rep this row until work measures 13cm. Change to 7½mm needles.
Next row: * K.2, inc. in next st. Rep. from * to end...80 sts. Now beg. with a p. row cont. in st.st. until back measures 41cm ending after a p. row. Join on B. Now still working in st.st. work from chart thus:
1st row: K., rep. 1st-12th sts. 6 times, then 1st-8th sts. once more.
2nd row: P. Work from 8th-1st once, then 12th-1st sts. 6 times. Cont. thus to follow chart until the 31 rows are completed. Break off C and cont. in A until work measures 61cm from beg. ending after a p. row.
Shape Shoulders:
Cast off 16 sts. at beg. of next 4 rows. Cast off rem. sts. loosely.
Right Front:
Using 5½mm needles and A cast on 36 sts. and work in twisted k.1, p.1 rib for 13cm. Change to 7½mm needles.
Next row: * K.4, inc. in next st. Rep. from * to last 4 sts., k.4...44 sts. Now beg. with a p. row cont. in st.st. until work measures 41cm

ending with a p. row. Join on B and follow 1st row of chart working 1st-12th sts. 3 times, then 1st-8th st. once. Cont. as for back until front measures 56cm ending after a p. row.
Shape Neck:
Cast off 6 sts. at beg. of next row, then cont. straight until work measures as back to shoulder ending at side edge.
Shape Shoulder:
Cast off 19 sts. at beg. of next 2 side edge rows.
Left Front
Work to match right front, reversing shapings.
SLEEVES.
Using A and 5½mm needles cast on 30 sts. and work in twisted rib for 7cm. Change to 7½mm needles.
Next row: K. twice into every st. to end...60 sts. Now beg. with a p. row cont. in st.st. until work measures 38cm ending with a p. row. Now work Fair Isle patt. working from row 31-20, thus working in reverse and repeating the 12 sts. 5 times across row. Cast off.
Left Front Band:
Using 5½mm needles and A cast on 12 sts. and work in twisted rib until band, slightly stretched measures as front to neck edge. Leave sts. on safety pin.
Right Front Band:
Place pins on left front band as a guide for button holes, 1st pin 4 rows up from lower edge, 2nd pin 13cm from top edge and 4 more at equal distances between. Using 5½mm needles and A cast on 12 sts. and work in twisted rib for 3 rows.
Next row: (right side) Rib 4, cast off 2, rib to end. In next row cast on 2 sts. in place of those cast off. Cont. in rib to match other band working button holes at pin position and ending after a wrong side row. Leave on spare needle.
Collar:
Join shoulders, easing in the fullness of front shoulder to corresponding back shoulder. Now using 5½mm needles and A, rib across the 12 sts. of right front band, pick up and k.12 sts. to neck edge, 14 sts. across back neck and 12 sts. down left front, then rib across the 12 sts. of left front band...62 sts. Work in twisted rib for 7 cm. Cast off in the rib loosely.
TO MAKE UP
Do not press. Sew in sleeves beg. and ending at Fair Isle patt. Now sew up sleeve and side seams. Sew on front bands, then sew on buttons to match button holes.

THE WAISTCOAT

Back:
Using 5½mm needles and A cast on 60 sts. and work in twisted rib for 10cm. Change to 7½mm needles and work front chart repeating the 12 sts. 5 times across, working rows 1-19, 3 times then rows 20-31 once. Break off C and cont. in A for a few rows until back measures 58cm. Cast off.
RIGHT FRONT:
Using 5½mm needles and A cast on 36 sts. and work as for back but rep. the 12 st. patt. 3 times across row and cont. until front measures 53cm ending after a p. row.

Shape Neck:
Cast off 12 sts. at beg. of next row, then cont. straight until front measures as back. Cast off.
LEFT FRONT:
Work to match right front reversing shapings.
Left Front Band:
Using 5½mm needles and A cast on 10 sts. and work in twisted rib until band slightly stretched measures as front to neck edge. Leave sts. on safety pin.
Right Front Band:
Place pins on left front band as a guide for button-holes, 1st pin 4 rows up from lower edge, 2nd in 9cm from top edge and 4 more at equal distances between. Using 5½mm needles and A cast on 10 sts. and work 3 rows in twisted rib.
Next row: (right side) Rib 6, cast off 2 sts., rib to end. In next row cast on 2 sts. in place of those cast off. Cont. in rib to match other band working button-holes at pin positions and ending after a wrong side row. Leave sts. on spare needle.
Neckband:
Join shoulders. Now using the 5½mm needles and A, rib across right front band sts., pick up and k.42 sts. up right front neck, across back and down left front then rib across left front band sts. Work in twisted rib over these 62 sts. for 4cm. Cast off in the rib loosely.
Armbands:
Using 5½mm needles and A cast on 10 sts. and work in twisted rib for 46cm with work slightly stretched. Cast off in the rib.
TO MAKE UP
Do not press. Sew on front bands neatly. Measure 23cm down from each shoulder at back and front and mark with pins. Sew on armbands between these 2 pins. Sew up side and armband seams. Sew on buttons to match button-holes.

□ = grey (A)
x = rust (B)
o = beige (C)

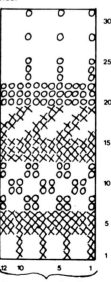

One repeat of pattern

ARGYLE SLIP-OVER

Materials: 3(3, 4, 4) 50g balls of Pingouin Confortable DK in grey. 1 50g ball of the same yarn in each of green, beige and coral-pink. A pair each of 3¾mm (Old No 9) and 3¼mm (Old No 10) knitting needles.

Measurements: To fit 86(92, 97, 102)cm – 34″(36″, 38″, 40″) bust or chest.
Length: 60(60, 61, 61)cm – 23½″(23½″, 24″, 24″).

Tension: 23 sts. and 30 rows measure 10cm (4″) over st.st. using 3¾mm needles.

Abbreviations: k, knit; p, purl; st.(s.), stitch(es); st.st., stocking stitch; beg., beginning; cont., continue; alt., alternate; dec., decrease; foll., following; inc., increase; patt., pattern; tog., together; tbl., through back of loop; rep., repeat; rem., remain(ing); m., main (grey); g., green; b., beige; c., coral-pink.

Size Note: Where 4 figures are given, follow 1st figures for 1st size, 2nd figures for 2nd size, 3rd figures for 3rd size and 4th figures for 4th size.

Metrication Note: Apart from measurements above no mention of inches is made in pattern.

Note: When working in Argyle patt. always twist yarns around each other on wrong side when changing from one colour to the next. For the 1st patt. you will need to wind off 2 small balls of g., and 1 ball of b. From the 5th row onwards you will also need 3 small balls of m. in addition to the main ball.

BACK
Using 3¼mm needles and m., cast on 106(110, 114, 122) sts. and work in rib thus:
1st row: (Right side) k.2, * p.2, k.2. Rep. from * to end.
2nd row: P.2, * k.2, p.2. Rep. from * to end.
Rep. these 2 rows until work measures 7cm, ending with a 1st rib row and inc. 1 st. each end of last row for 2nd and 3rd sizes only. Change to 3¾mm needles and p. one row on these 106(112, 116, 122) sts. Now work in patt. thus:
1st row: K.18(21, 23, 26) m., join on g., k.2 g, then 32 m., join on b., k.2 b., then k.32 m., join on g., k.2 g, then 18(21, 23, 26) m.
2nd and alt. rows: P. with colours as set twisting them when changing.
3rd row: K.17 (20, 22, 25) m., 4 g., 30 m., 4 b., 30 m., 4 g., 17(20, 22, 25) m.
5th row: K.16(19, 21, 24) m., twist colours and leave m. hanging, k.6 g., join on 2nd ball of m., k.28 m., twist colours and leave m. hanging, k.6 b., join on 3rd ball of m., k.28 m., twist colours, and leave m. hanging, k.6 g., join on another ball of m., k.16(19, 21, 24) m.

7th row: K.15(18, 20, 23) m., 8 g., 26 m., 8 b., 26 m., 8 g., 15(18, 20, 23) m. Cont. thus working 2 sts. more in each diamond on every k. row with 2 sts. less in m. between them, and 1 st. less in m. at each side edge until the 31st and 32nd rows have been worked with 32 sts. in g. and b. diamonds.
33rd and 34th rows: 2(5, 7, 10) m., 34 g., 34 b., 34 g., 2(5, 7, 10) m.
35th row: 3(5, 8, 11) m., 32 g., 2 m., 32 b., 2 m., 32 g., 3(6, 8, 11) m. Cont. working 2 sts. less in each diamond on every k. row until the 65th and 66th rows, which were as 1st and 2nd rows, have been worked. This completes one patt. Cut b. and g. and beg. 2nd patt. which has a different arrangement of colours.
1st row: K.18(21, 23, 26) m., join on b., k.2 b, then 32 m., join on c., k.2 c., then 32 m., join on b., k.2 b., then 18(21,23,26) m.
Cont. working as for 1st patt, with colours as now set until work measures 39cm from beg. ending with a p. row.
Shape Armholes:
Keeping continuity of patt,, cast off 3 sts. at beg. of next 2 rows, 2 sts. at beg. of next 8 rows and 1 st. at beg. of next 8(10, 10, 12) rows. Cont. on rem. 76(80, 84, 88) sts. and when 2nd patt. is completed beg. new diamonds in same colours as for 1st patt. keeping in line with previous diamond. Cont. straight until work measures 60(60, 61, 61)cm from beg. ending with a p. row.
Shape Shoulder and Neck:
1st row: Cast off 6 sts., patt. until there are 22(24, 25, 27) sts. on right-hand needle, leave these for right back, cast off next 20(20, 22, 22) sts., patt. to end. Cont. on 28(30, 31, 33) sts. now rem. on needle for left back. Cast off 6 sts. at beg. of next row and 5 sts. at neck edge on foll. row. Rep. last 2 rows once more. Cast off rem. 6(8, 9, 11) sts. Go back to other sts., and with wrong side of work facing, rejoin yarn to neck edge of right back sts., cast off 5 sts., patt. to end. Cast off 6 sts. at beg. of next row and 5 sts. at neck edge on foll. row. Cast off rem. 6(8, 9, 11) sts.
FRONT
Work as for Back but reversing colours of diamonds so that on 1st patt. the first diamond is in b., centre one in g. and the third in b. and on 2nd patt. the first diamond is in c., then the centre one in b., and the third in c. Cont. thus in patt. until 6 rows less than Back to beg. of armhole shaping, thus ending after a p. row.
Shape Neck and Armhole
Next row: Patt. 53(56, 58, 61) sts., turn and cont. on these sts. Leave rem. sts. on a spare needle. Now dec. 1 st. at neck edge on next 10(10, 11, 11) alt. rows then at same edge on every foll. 4th row 10 times, *but at the same time* keep side edge straight for 5 more rows, then cast off at this edge 3 sts. on

next row, 2 sts. on next 4 alt. rows and 1 st. on next 4(5, 5, 6) alt. rows. Cont. straight at armhole edge, still dec. as given at neck edge until 18(20, 21, 23) sts. rem., then cont. until work measures as Back to shoulder, ending at armhole edge.
Shape Shoulder:
Cast off 6 sts. at beg. of next row and foll. alt. row. Work one row, then cast off rem. 6(8, 9, 11) sts. Go back to other sts., rejoin yarn to neck edge of right front sts., patt. to end. Now work to match other side, reversing all shapings.
FRONT NECKBAND
Using 3¼mm needles and with right side of work facing and m., pick up and k. 61(61, 63, 63) sts. down left front neck and 61(61, 63, 63) sts. up right front neck. Rep. 2nd(2nd, 1st, 1st) rib row thus giving a k.2 rib at centre front on right side rows.
Next row: (Right side) Rib 58(58, 60, 60) sts., p.2 tog. tbl., k.2, p.2 tog., rib 58(58, 60, 60).
Next row: Rib to 2 sts. before centre 2 sts., k.2 tog., p.2, k.2 tog. tbl., rib to end. Cont. to dec. thus on next 6 rows keeping continuity of rib. Cast off in the rib.
BACK NECKBAND
With right side of work facing and using 3¼mm needles and m., pick up and k.46(46, 50, 50) sts. across Back neck and beg. with 2nd(2nd, 1st, 1st) rib row work 9 rows in rib as on welt. Cast off in the rib.
ARMBANDS
Join shoulders and ends of neckbands. Now with right side of work facing and using 3¼mm needles and m., pick up and k.118(118, 122, 122) sts. all round armhole edge. Beg. with a 2nd row work 7 rows in rib. Cast off ribwise but at underarm curved edge, p.2 tog. on the p.2 rib, 3 times each side to give a neat edge.
TO MAKE UP
Press work lightly on wrong side with a warm iron over a damp cloth. Sew up side seams and armbands' edges. Press seams, using the point of the iron.

31

PASTEL PLAID CARDIGAN

Materials: 8(9,9) 50g balls of Sirdar Majestic Luxury Pure New Wool Double Knitting in Main colour. 2 (2,3) balls of the same yarn in first and second contrasting colours. A pair each of 4mm (old No 8) and 3¼mm (old No 10) knitting needles. A 3.50mm (old No 9) crochet hook. 6 buttons.

Measurements: To fit 86(91, 97) cm or 34 (36", 38") bust. Length from shoulder, 63 (63.5, 63.5) cm 24¾ (25", 25"). Sleeve seam, 43cm (17").

Tension: 11½ sts. measures 5cm (2") over patt.

Abbreviations: k., knit; p., purl; sts., stitch(es); rep., repeat; patt., pattern; beg., beginning; inc., increase; dec., decrease; rem., remain(ing); cont., continue; M., main colour, C., contrasting colour.

Size Note: Where 3 figures are given, follow 1st figures for 1st size, 2nd figures for 2nd size and 3rd figures for 3rd size.

Metrication note: Except for measurements above no reference to inches is made in pattern.

BACK
Using 3¼mm needles and M. cast on 107(113, 119) sts. and work 6cm in k.1 p.1 rib beg. alternate rows p.1. Change to 4mm needles and patt. thus:

1st row: k.4 (7, 10), p.1, k.1, p.1, * k.13, p.1, k.1, p.1. Rep. from * to last 4(7, 10) sts., k.4 (7, 10).

2nd row: P.

These 2 rows form the patt. Rep. last 2 rows once more. Joining and breaking colours as required, rep. the 2 patt. rows throughout and work in stripes of 2 rows 1st C., 2 rows M., 4 rows 2nd C. 2 rows M. 2 rows 1st C. and 18 rows M. These 30 rows form the stripe patt. Cont. in patt. until Back measures 43cm or length required. If a different length is worked, then this must be allowed for in shoulder and neck shaping.

Shape Armholes:
Keeping continuity of patt. and stripes, cast off 6 sts. at beg. of next 2 rows, then dec. 1 st. at both ends of every row until 83(89, 93) sts. rem. Cont. straight until back measures 63(63.5, 63.5) cm.

Shape Shoulders.
Cast off 8(9, 9) sts. at beg. of next 4 rows and 8(8, 10) sts. at beg. of following 2 rows. Slip rem. 35(37, 37) sts. on a st. holder.

LEFT FRONT
Using 3¼mm needles and M. cast on 52(55, 58) sts. and work 6cm in k.1, p.1 rib, for 2nd size beg. alternate rows p.1.

Change to 4mm needles and patt. thus:

1st row: k.4 (7, 10), * p.1, k.1, p.1, k.13. Rep from * to end.

2nd row: P.

These 2 rows form the patt. for left front. Rep. last 2 rows once more, then cont. in stripe patt. as for Back. Work straight until front measures as Back to armholes, ending at side edge.

Shape Armhole:
Cast off 6 sts. at beg. of next row, then dec. 1 st. at armhole edge on every row until 40(43, 45) sts. rem. Cont. straight until front measures 55(56, 56) cm ending at front edge.

Shape Neck:
1st row: P.6 and slip these sts. on a safety pin for neck border, P. to end. Dec.1 st. at neck edge on every row until 24(26, 28) sts. rem. Cont. straight until same length as Back to shoulder, ending at armhole edge.

Shape Shoulder:
Cast off 8(9, 9) sts. at beg. of next and following alternate row. Work 1 row. Cast off rem. 8(8, 10) sts.

THE RIGHT FRONT
Work as Left Front, but reading patt. instead of P. on 1st neck shaping row and working main patt. thus:

1st row: * K.13, p.1, k.1, p.1. Rep from * to last 4(7, 10) sts., k.4 (7, 10)

2nd row: P. These 2 rows form the patt. for Right Front.

THE SLEEVES
Using 3¼mm needles and M., cast on 52 sts. and work 6cm in k.1, p.1 rib, ending with a right side row.

Inc. row: * Rib 2, inc. in next st. Rep. from * to last st., rib 1 . . . 69 sts. Change to 4mm needles and patt. thus:

1st row: (k.1, p.1) twice, * k.13, p.1, k.1, p.1. Rep from * to last st., k.1.

2nd row: P. Rep. last 2 rows once more, then cont. in patt. as set, working in stripes as for Back and inc. 1 st. each end of 17th and every following 18th (16th, 16th) row until there are 79(81, 81) sts. Cont. straight until sleeve measures as front to armholes ending after the same row.

Shape Top
Cast off 6 sts. at beg. of next 2 rows. Dec. 1 st. at beg. of every row until 29 sts. rem., then dec. 1 st. at each end of every row until 21 sts. rem. Cast off.

THE VERTICAL STRIPES
Using crochet hook, work vertical stripes of chain sts. up each row of p. sts., begin at 1st p. row from front edges of fronts and work towards side edge thus: Work 1 row 2nd C., 1 row 1st C. up first panel and 1 row 1st C. and 1 row 2nd C. up second panel, 1 row 2nd C. and 1 row 1st C. up

third panel. Begin at right side edge of Back, work * 1 row 2nd C., 1 row 1st C., 1 row 1st C. and 1 row 2nd C. Rep from * twice more, work 1 row 2nd C and 1 row 1st C. Work sleeves to match.

TO MAKE UP
Press, omitting ribbing. Join shoulder seams.

The Neckborder: Using 3¼mm needles and M. k. across 6 sts. of right front (left on safety pin), pick up and k.20 (21, 21) sts. up right side of neck, k. across sts. from Back neck, pick up and k.20 (21, 21) sts. down left side of neck and k. across 6 sts. from safety pin. Work 7 rows in rib as for Back. Cast off in rib.

The Right Front Border. Using 3¼mm needles and M. pick up and k. 147(149, 149) sts. up right front edge, ending at top edge of neck border. Work 3 rows in rib as for Back.

Buttonhole Row: Rib 6(3, 3) cast off 3 sts., * rib 24(25, 25) cast off 3 sts. Rep from * 4 times more, rib to end. Work another 5 rows in rib, casting on 3 sts. over those cast off in 1st row. Cast off in rib.

The Left Front Border: Work as for right front border, but begin picking up sts. at top edge of neckborder and omitting buttonholes. Join side and sleeve seams. Sew in sleeves. Press seams, then sew on buttons.

PAISLEY PULLOVER IN MOHAIR

Materials: 13(13, 13) 25g balls of Hayfield Gossamer in White. 1 ball of same yarn in Sky Blue and Rust. A pair of 5mm (Old No 6) and 6mm (Old No 4) knitting needles. Darning needle for Swiss Darning.

Measurements: To fit 86(91, 97)cm – 34"(36", 38") bust. Length to back of neck, 55(56, 57)cm – 21½"(22", 22½"). Sleeve seam, 43(43, 44)cm – 17"(17", 17½") adjustable.

Tension: 8 sts. and 10 rows to 5cm (2") over st. st.

Abbreviations: K., knit; p., purl; st.(s), stitch(es); st. st., stocking stitch; inc., increase; dec., decrease; rep., repeat; alt., alternate; foll., following; beg., beginning; tog., together; rem., remain(ing); cont., continue; patt., pattern; M, main; W, white; B, blue; R, rust.

Size note: Where 3 figures are given, follow 1st figures for 1st size, 2nd figures for 2nd size and 3rd figures for 3rd size.

Metrication Note: Apart from measurements above no mention of inches is made in pattern.

Knitting Note: To avoid stranding at the back of work, use separate balls of wool, twisting yarns around each other when changing colours. All linear details in R and W on back and front of jumper are embroidered in Swiss darning. The motifs on sleeves are Swiss darned.

BACK

Using 5mm needles and M, cast on 60(64, 66) sts. and work in k.1, p.1 rib for 7.5cm.

Next row: * Rib 2 inc. in next st. Rep. from * 19(19, 21) times, rib 0(4,0) . . . 80(84, 88) sts. Change to 6mm needles and work in st. st. for 10(12, 12) rows,

then cont. in st. st. placing motifs from charts thus:

Next row: K.52(54, 56)M, 4B, 24(26, 28)M. Complete motif from chart A. Work 3 rows in st. st. in M. Work motif B. thus:

Next row: K.26(28, 30)M, 1B, 53(55, 57)M. Complete motif from chart. Work 3 rows in st. st. in M. 47(49, 49) rows have now been worked in st. st from welt. Work motif C from chart thus:

Next row: P.24(26, 28)M, 6B, 50(52, 54)M. Cont. to work 10 more rows from chart.

Shape Armholes:
Keeping continuity of chart patt., cast off 8(9, 10) sts. at beg. of next 2 rows. Now dec. 1 st. each end of next and foll. 5 alt. rows, *but at the same time* working 3 rows in st. st. in M when chart C is completed and placing chart D thus: K.2 tog., k.14(16, 18)M, 3B, 37(39, 41)M, k.2 tog. When decs. and motif are completed, cont. in st. st. until work measures 55(56, 57)cm from beg.

Shape Shoulders:
Cast off 7(7, 8) sts. at beg. of next 2 rows, and 7(8, 8) sts. at beg. of next 2 rows. Leave rem. 24 sts. on a spare needle.

FRONT

Work as for Back until 7 rows of Chart D have been worked after armhole shaping is completed.

Shape Neck
Next row: Patt. 21, turn and leave rem. 31(33, 35) sts. on st. holder. Keeping continuity of chart, work on neck sts. thus:

Dec. 1 st. at neck edge on next row and foll. 7(6, 5) alt. rows. Cont. straight until front measures as Back to shoulder shaping ending at armhole edge.

Shape Shoulder:
Cast off 7(7, 8) sts. at beg. of next row, p. one row, then cast off rem. 7(8, 8) sts. Go

back to sts. left on st. holder, leave centre 10(12,14) sts. on holder, and work on rem. sts. to match other side, reversing shapings.

SLEEVES

Using 5mm needles and M cast on 30(32, 34) sts. and work in k.1, p.1 rib for 7.5cm.

Next row: * K.1, inc. in next st., k.1. Rep. from * to last 3(5, 7), k.1, inc. in next st., k.1(3, 5) . . . 40(42, 44) sts. Change to 6mm needles and work in st. st. inc. 1 st each end of every 6th row until there are 60(62, 64) sts. Cont. straight until work measures 43(43, 44)cm or length required, ending after a p. row.

Shape Top:
Cast off 8(9, 10) sts. at beg. of next 2 rows, then dec. 1 st. each end of next and every foll. 3rd row until 20(20, 18)sts. rem.

Next row: K.4(4, 3) tog., 5(5, 6) times. Cast off rem. sts.

NECKBAND

Join right shoulders together. Now using 5mm needles and with right side of work facing, and M, pick up and k.15 sts. down left front neck, 10(12, 14) sts. from front st. holder, pick up and k.15 sts. up right front neck, then k. across the 24 sts. from back spare needle . . . 64(66, 68) sts. Work in k.1, p.1 rib for 6cm. Cast off loosely in the rib.

SWISS DARNING

First join left shoulder and neck seams. Now with R and a darning needle Swiss darn around the shapes where indicated on the charts, thus: bring needle up through the st. below the one to be covered, then pass it under the st. above the one to be covered, then pass back down through the same st. it came up through in the first place. Using B complete motif. For sleeves use R as indicated on motifs A and D placing motif A on 17th row of sleeve thus: Swiss darn over 19th, 20th, 21st and 22nd sts. from right side edge. This places base of motif A on sleeve. Complete following chart, but using B for the V and noting that background is therefore W. Place base of motif D thus: on 6th row before sleeve top shaping, Swiss darn over 31st, 32nd and 33rd sts. from right side edge. Complete from chart using B for W.

TO MAKE UP

Do not press. Sew up sleeve and side seams. Sew in sleeves.

BACK AND FRONTS ONLY

- ■ RUST – TO BE SWISS DARNED
- ▨ WHITE – TO BE SWISS DARNED
- ▣ BLUE – TO BE KNITTED

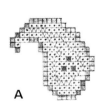 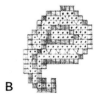  

A   B   C   D

Materials: 12 50g (2 oz) balls of 3 Suisses Suizastar for dress, and 1 ball for headband. A pair of 3¼mm (old No 10) knitting needles. A long pair of 4mm (old No 8) knitting needles. 2½cm (1") wide elastic to fit bust measurement.

Measurement: To fit a 81-87 (91-97)cm – 32"-34" (36"-38") bust.

Tension: 6 sts. and 8 rows measure 2½cm (1") using 3¼mm needles over st.st.

Note: The bodice of the dress will appear to be very long and narrow. This is deliberate, to use the stretch of the knitting to give a tight, smooth fit.

Abbreviations: k., knit; p., purl; st(s)., stitch(es); st.st., stocking stitch; cm, centimetres; cont., continue; rep., repeat; beg., beginning; inc., increase or increasing; yfwd., yarn forward to make a stitch; tog., together.

Size Note: Where 2 figures are given, follow 1st figures for 1st size and figures in brackets for 2nd size.

Metrification Note: Apart from measurements above no mention of inches is made in pattern.

DRESS
BACK AND FRONT ALIKE
Using 3¼mm needles cast on 153(159) sts. and work 30cm in st.st. ending after a p. row.

Next row: K.2 tog. all along row to last st., k.1 77(80) sts. Cont. straight for another 42cm – or length required – ending with a p. row. Work measures 72cm from beg.

Next row (picot edge): K.2, * k.2 tog., yfwd. rep. from * to last 3(2) sts., k. to end.

Work 2½cm in st.st. Cast off loosely.

FRILL (Make 6)
Using 4mm needles cast on 153(159) sts. and work 2 rows in st.st.

Next row: K. inc. in every st. 306(318) sts.

Next row: P.

Cont. in pattern thus:

1st row: K.1, * yfwd., k.2 tog. Rep. from * to last st., k.1.

2nd row: P.

Rep. these 2 rows until work measures 13cm from beg. ending after a p. row. Now beg. with a p. row work 6 rows in reverse st.st. thus ending after a k. row.

In next row cast off making picot point thus:

* Insert right-hand needle through first st.; cast on 2 sts.; then cast off these 2 sts.; k. next st. (There are now 2 sts. on right-hand needle.) Cast off first of these 2 sts., return remaining st. to left-hand needle, k. st. again, and cast off this st. and following st. Return st. to left-hand needle. Rep. from * to end. Fasten off last st.

TO MAKE UP
Press frills lightly. (Do not press back and

CHRISTMAS WRAPPING IN LUREX

---

front of dress.) Sew frills on to skirt of dress, 1st one beg. at lower edge, 2nd one at decrease line of skirt and 3rd one between 1st and 2nd frill. Join side and frill seams. Fold over hem at picot edge at top of dress and slipstitch neatly in place. Thread elastic through to fit.

HEADBAND
Band: Using 3¼mm needles cast on 100 sts. and work 6 rows in st.st. ending with a p. row.

Next row (picot row): K.1, * k.2 tog., yfwd. Rep. from * to last st., k.1. Beg. with a p. row work 11 rows in st.st. thus ending with a p. row. Work picot row once more, then work 6 rows in st.st. Cast off.

Bow Trim: Using 3¼mm needles cast on 24 sts. and work 16 rows in st.st.

Next row: Work picot row as for Band. Work 29 rows in st.st.

Work picot row as before, then work 16 rows st.st. Cast off.

TO MAKE UP
Fold band along picot edges and hem down neatly. Fold bow along picot edge and join. Now run a gathering thread through centre of bow and wrap around several times to secure. Sew bow on to band. Join ends of band.

AZTEC JACKET

Materials: 20 50g (2 oz) balls in Sirdar Sportswool consisting of 15 balls in Terra Cotta (M), 2 balls in each of Navy and Red and 1 ball in Gold. A pair each of 3¼mm (Old No 9) and 4mm (Old No 8) knitting needles. Cable needle.

Measurements: To fit a 87(91,97)cm – 34"(36",38") bust. Length from top shoulder: 71cm (28"). Sleeve seam: 51cm (20") adjustable.

Tension: 10 sts. and 14 rows measure 5cm (2").

Abbreviations: k., knit; p., purl; st.(s), stitch(es); st.st., stocking stitch; cont., continue; foll., following; rep., repeat; beg., beginning; patt., pattern; cm, centimetres; cb 3(4), cable 3(4) sts., ie, slip next 3(4) sts. on cable needle and leave at front of work, k. next 3(4) sts., then k. sts. from cable needle.

Size Note: Where 3 figures are given, foll. 1st figures for 1st size, 2nd figures for 2nd size and 3rd figures for 3rd size.

Metrication Note: Apart for above no mention of inches is made in pattern.

BACK: Using 3¾mm needles and M., cast on 94(100, 104) sts. and work in k.2, p.2 rib for 9 rows. Change to 4mm needles and beg. with a p. row, work 4 rows in reversed st.st. (p. side is right side). Cont. in patt.

5th row: p.9(12, 14) M *, k.2 N, p.2 M, k.2 N, p.4 M, k.2 R, p.2 M, k.2 R * p.44 M, Rep. from * to *, p.9(12, 14) M.

6th row: k.9(12, 14) M *, k.2 R, p.2 R, k.4 M, p.2 N, k.2 M, p.2 N * k.44 M. Rep. from * to *, k.9(12, 14) M.

Unless stated all wrong side rows, k. in main colour and p. all other sts.

Rep. 5th and 6th rows twice more.

11th row: p.6(9, 11) M, k.11 N, k.11 R, p.38 M, k.11 N, k.11 R, p.6(9, 11) M.

13th row: p.7(10, 12) M, k.10 N, k.10 R, p.40 M, k.10 N, k.10 R, p.7(10, 12) M.

15th row: p.8(11, 13) M, k.9 N, k.9 R, p.42 M, k.9 N, k.9 R, p.8(11, 13) M.

Cont. in this way until the row beg. k.12(15, 17) M, p.5 N, has been worked.

25th row: p.13(16, 18) M, k.4 N, k.4 R, p.22 M, k.8 G, p.22 M, k.4 N, k.4 R, p.13(16, 18) M.

27th row: p.14(17, 19) M, k.3 N, k.3 R, p.23 M, k.8 G, p.23 M, k.3 N, k.3 R, p.14(17, 19) M.

29th row: p.15(18, 20) M, k.2 N, k.2 R, p.24 M, k.8 G, p.24 M, k.2 N, k.2 R, p.15(18, 20) M.

31st row: p.16(19, 21) M, k.1 N, k.1 R, p.25 M, cb4 G, p.25 M, k.1 N, k.1 R, p.16(19, 21) M.

32nd row: (Reverse colours for triangle) k.16(19, 21) M, p.1 N, p.1 R, k.25 M, p.8 G, k.25 M, p.1 N, p.1 R, k.16(19, 21) M.

33rd row: p.15(18, 20) M, k.2 R, k.2 N, p.24 M, k.8 G, p.24 M, k.2 R, k.2 N, p.15(18, 20) M.

35th row: p.14(17, 19) M, k.3 R, k.3 N, p.23 M, k.8 G, p.23 M, k.3 R, k.3 N, p.14(17, 19) M.

37th row: p.13(16, 18) M, k.4 R, k.4 N, p.22 M, k.8 G, p.22 M, k.4 R, k.4 N, p.13(16, 18) M.

Cont. triangle as before until row 52 which begins k.6(9, 11) M, p.11 N, p.11 R has been completed.

53rd row: p.6(9, 11) M, k.3 M *, k.2 R, k.2 M, k.2 R, k.4 M, k.2 N, k.2 M, k.2 N * k.3 M, p.38 M, k.3 M. Rep. from * to *, k.3 M, p.6(9, 11) M.

54th row: k. main colour, p. all others.

55th row: p.9(12, 14) M *, k.2 R, p.2 M, k.2 R, p.4 M, k.2 N, p.2 M, k.2 N *, p.44 M. Rep. from * to *, p.9(12, 14) M.

Rep. rows 54 and 55, then 54th row.

59th row: p.9(12, 14) M, k.2 M, p.2 M, k.2 M *, p.4 M. Rep. from * to *, p.14 M, k.2 R, p.2 M, k.2 R, p.4 M, k.2 N, p.2 M, k.2 N, p.14 M *. Rep. from * to *, p.4 M, rep. from * to *, p.9(12, 14) M.

61st row: p.39(42, 44) M, k.2 R, p.2 M, k.2 R, p.4 M, k.2 N, p.2 N, k.2 N, p.39(42, 44) M.

Rep. rows 60 and 61 then 60th row.

65th row: p.36(39, 41) M, k.11 R, k.11 N, p.36(39, 41) M.

67th row: p.37(40, 42) M, k.10 R, k.10 N, p.37(40, 42) M.

69th row: p.38(41, 43) M, k.9 R, k.9 N, p.38(41, 43) M.

Cont. triangle until the 78th row which began k.42(45, 46) M, p.5 R, p.5 N has been worked.

79th row: p.13(16, 18) M, k.8 G, p.22 M, k.4 R, k.4 N, p.22 M, k.8 G, p.13(16, 18) M.

81st row: p.13(16, 18) M, k.8 G, p.23 M, k.3 R, k.3 N, p.23 M, k.8 G, p.13(16, 18) M.

83rd row: p.13(16, 18) M, k.8 G, p.24 M, k.2 R, k.2 N, p.24 M, k.8 G, p.13(16, 18) M.

85th row: p.13(16, 18) M, cb4 G, p.25 M, k.1 R, k.1 N, p.25 M, cb4 G, p.13(16, 18) M.

86th row: (Reverse colours) k.13(16, 18) M, p.8 G, k.25 M, p.1 R, p.1 N, k.25 M, p.8 G, k.13(16, 18) M.

87th row: p.13(16, 18) M, k.8 G, p.24 M, k.2 N, k.2 R, p.24 M, k.8 G, p.13(16, 18) M.

89th row: p.13(16, 18) M, k.8 G, p.23 M, k.3 N, k.3 R, p.23 M, k.8 G, p.13(16, 18) M.

91st row: p.13(16, 18) M, k.8 M, p.22 M, k.4 N, k.4 R, p.22 M, k.8 M, p.13(16, 18) M.

93rd row: p.42(45, 47) M, k.5 N, k.5 R, p.42(45, 47) M.

95th row: p.41(44, 46) M, k.6 N, k.6 R, p.41(44, 46) M.

Cont. triangle until the 106th row which began k.36(39, 41) M, k.11 R, k.11 N has been completed.

107th row: p.36(39, 41) M, k.3 M, k.2 N, k.2 M, k.2 N, k.4 M, k.2 R, k.2 M, k.2 R, k.3 M, p.36(39, 41) M.

109th row: p.39(42, 44) M, k.2 N, p.2 M, k.2 M, k.2 N, p.4 M, k.2 R, p.2 M, k.2 R, p.39(42, 44) M.

Rep. rows 108 amd 109 then 108th row.

113th row: p.9(12, 14) M *, k.2 N, p.2 M, k.2 N, p.4 M, k.2 R, p.2 M, k.2 R *, p.14 M, k.2 M, k.2 N, p.4 M, k.2 M, k.2 R, p.2 M, k.2 M, p.2 M, k.2 M, p.14 M. Rep. from * to *, p.9(12, 14) M.

Rep. rows 6 to 58 inclusive.

Next row: Using M, p.9(12, 14) *, k.2, p.2, k.2, p.4, k.2, p.2, k.2 *, p.44. Rep. from * to *, p.9(12, 14).

Work 3 rows in reverse st.st., then cast off 17 sts. at beg. of next 4 rows. Cast off rem. sts.

LEFT FRONT: Using 3¾mm needles and M. cast on 50(51,52) sts. and work in k.2, p.2 rib for 9 rows. Change to 4mm needles and work 4 rows in st.st.

5th row: p.9(10, 11) M, k.2 N, p.2 M, k.2 N, p.4 M, k.2 R, p.2 M, k.2 R, p.25 M. Cont. in patt. as set to match Back, until 24 rows have been worked.

25th row: p.13(14, 15) M, k.4 N, k.4 R, p.8 M, k.8 G, p.13 M.

27th row: p.14(15, 16) M, k.3 N, k.3 R, p.9 M, k.8 G, p.13 M.

29th row: p.15(16, 17) M, k.2 N, k.2 R, p.10 M, k.8 G, p.13 M.

31st row: p.16(17, 18) M, k.1 N, k.1 R, p.11 M, cb4 G, p.13 M.

32nd row: (reverse colours): k.13 M, p.8 G, k.11 M, p.1 N, p.1 R, k.16(17, 18) M.

33rd row: p.15(16, 17) M, k.2 R, k.2 N, p.10 M, k.8 G, p.13 M.

35th row: p.14(15, 16) M, k.3 R, k.3 N, p.9 M, k.8 G, p.13 M.

37th row: p.13(14, 15) M, k.4 R, k.4 N, p.8 M, k.8 G, p.13 M.

Now cont. in patt. until 58 rows are complete, matching Back.

59th row: p.9(10, 11) M, (k.2, p.2, k.2, p.4, k.2, p.2, k.2) M, k.2 R, p.2 M, k.2 R, p.4 M, k.2 N, p.2 M, k.2 N, p.9 M.

60th row: k. M colour, p. all others.
61st row: p.25(26, 27) M, k.2 R, p.2 M, k.2 R, p.4 M, k.2 N, p.2 M, k.2 N, p.9 M. Rep. rows 60 and 61, then 60th row again.
65th row: p.22(23, 24) M, k.11 R, k.11 N, p.6 M.
67th row: p.23(24, 25) M, k.10 R, k.10 N, p.7 M.
69th row: p.24(25, 26) M, k.9 R, k.9 N, p.8 N.
Work until row k.28(29, 30) M, p.5 N, p.5 R, k.12 M is complete.
79th row: p.13(14, 15) M, k.8 G, p.8 M, k.4 R, k.4 N, p.13 M.
81st row: p.13(14, 15) M, k.8 G, p.9 M, k.3 R, k.3 N, p.14 M.
83rd row: p.13(14, 15) M, k.8 G, p.10 M, k.2 R, k.2 N, p.15 M.
85th row: p.13(14, 15) M, cb4 G, p.11 M, k.1 R, k.1 N, p.16 M.
86th row (reverse colour triangle): k.16 M, p.1 R, p.1 N, k.11 M, p.8 G, k.13(14, 15) M.
87th row: p.13(14, 15) M, k.8 G, p.10 M, k.2 R, k.2 N, p.15 M.
89th row: p.13(14, 15) M, k.8 G, p.9 M, k.3 N, k.3 R, p.14 M.
91st row: p.13(14, 15) M, k.8 M, p.8 M, k.4 N, k.4 R, p.13 M.
93rd row: p.28(29, 30) M, k.5 M, k.5 R, p.12 M.
95th row: p.27(28, 29) M, k.6 N, k.6 R, p.11 M.
Cont. triangle until row k.6 M, p.11 R, p.11 N, k.22(23, 24) M is complete.
Next row: p.22(23, 24) M, k.3 M, k.2 N, k.2 M, k.2 N, k.4 M, k.2 R, k.2 M, k.2 R, k.3 M, p.6 M.
Next row: k. M colour, p. all others.
Next row: p.25(26, 27) M, k.2 N, p.2 M, k.2 N, p.4 M, k.2 R, p.2 M, k.2 R, p.9 M. Rep. last 2 rows once, then 1st row again.
Next row: p.9(10, 11) M, k.2 N, p.2 M, k.2 N, p.4 M, k.2 R, p.2 M, k.2 R, (k.2, p.2, k.2, p.4, k.2, p.2, k.2) M. p.9 M.
Rep. 6th-57th row (inclusive) – (Note 6th-58th row on Right Front)
Next row: cast off 6 sts., patt. to end.
Next row: in patt.
Next row: cast off 2 sts. k. to end.

Next row: p.
Next row: cast off 3 sts. k. to end.
Next row: cast off 17 sts., p. to end.
Next row: cast off 3 sts., k. to end.
Next row: cast off 17 sts., p. to end. Cast off remaining 2 sts.
RIGHT FRONT: Work to match left front, reversing position of patts, therefore 5th row will read: p.25 M, k.2 N, p.2 M, k.2 N, p.4 M, k.2 R, p.2 M, k.2 R, p.9(10, 11) M.
59th row will read: p.9 M, k.2 R, p.2 M, k.2 R, p.4 M, k.2 N, p.2 M, k.2 N (k.2, p.2, k.2, p.4, k.2, p.2, k.2) M, p.9(10, 11) M.
SLEEVES: Using 3¾mm needles and M. cast on 50 sts. for each size and work in k.2, p.2 rib for 9 rows. Change to 4mm needles and work 22 rows in st.st. inc. 1 st. each end of 4th and every foll. 6th row. Keeping continuity of incs. cont. thus:
23rd row: p.25 M, k.8 G, p.25 M.
24th row: k.25 M, p.8 G, k.25 M.
Rep. rows 24 and 25 twice, but inc. 1 st. each end of last row.
29th row: p.26 M, cb4 G, p.26 M . . . 60 sts.
30th row: k.26 M, p.8 G, k.26 M.
31st row: p.26 M. k.8 G, p.26 M.
Rep. rows 30 and 31 once more then 30th row (inc. row) again.
35th row: p.27 M, k.8 M, p.27 M.
Using M. work 19 rows in reversed st.st. . . . 68 sts.
55th row: p.26 M, k.2 R, p.2 M, k.2 R, p.4 M, k.2 N, p.2 M, k.2 N, p.26 M.
56th row: k. M. colour, p. all others.
Rep. rows 55 and 56 twice more, allowing for inc. sts each end of 58th row.
61st row: p.24 M, k.11 R, k.11 N, p.24 M.
Cont. triangle until row k.32 M, p.5 N, p.5 R, k.32 M is complete.
75th row: p.14 M, k.8 G, p.11 M, k.4 R, k.4 N, p.11 M, k.8 G, p.14 M.
76th row: (inc. row) k. M. colour, p. all others.
Cont. triangle and Gold as before.
81st row: p.15 M, cb4 G, p.14 M, k.1 R, k.1 N, p.14 M, cb4 G, p.15 M.
82nd row: (inc. row) Inc. in 1st.st., k.14

M, p.8 G, k.14 M, p.1 R, p.1 N, k.14 M, p.8 G, k.14, inc. in last st. Complete triangle and Gold as before.
109th row: (p.35, k.2, p.2, k.2, p.4, k.2, p.2, k.2, p.35) M.
Work 15 rows reversed st.st. inc. on rows 112 and 118. Cast off loosely.
FRONT BANDS (two alike): Using 3¾mm needles and M. cast on 8 sts. k.1 row, p.1 row. Patt. thus:
1st row: k.4 M, k.3 G, k.1 M.
2nd row: k.1 M, p.3 G, p.3 M, k.1 M.
Rep. last 2 rows 3 times.
9th row: k.1 M, cb3 G, k.1 M.
10th row: k.1 M, p.3 M, p.3 G, k.1 M.
11th row: k.1 M. k.3 G, k.4 M.
12th row: k.1 M, p.3 M, p.3 G, k.1 M.
Rep. last 2 rows 3 times more.
19th row: k.1 M, cb3, k.1 M.
20th row: k.1 M, p.3 G, p.3 M, k.1 M.
Rep. these 20 rows until band measures 66 cm. Cast off.
COLLAR: Using 3¾mm needles and M. cast on 12 sts.
1st row: k.6 M, k.3 G, k.3 M.
2nd row: k.3 M, p.3 G, p.3 M, k.3 M.
Rep. last 2 rows twice more.
7th row: k.3 M, cb3, k.3 M
8th row: As 2nd row.
Keeping 3 sts. each end in garter st. cont. in patt. until long enough to fit neck. Cast off.

Collar Lining
Using 3¾mm needles and M. cast on 10 sts. work in st.st., slipping 1st st. of every row until piece measures as collar. Cast off.

TO MAKE UP
Press work on wrong side, pressing cables lightly. Join shoulder side and sleeve seams. Sew in sleeves, Sew short edges of collar and collar lining together, right sides facing. Turn to right side. Sew lining in position just below collar edge. Sew on collar. Stitch front bands on top of the knitting on either side of front opening – this gives a firm edge. Lastly make tassels in red and sew to two ends of each navy triangle, then work tassels in navy and sew to red triangles.

STAR-SPANGLED JACKET

Materials: Of Sirdar Wash 'n' Wear DK: 31 balls in Light Navy No 224, two balls Royal (No 273) and one ball each of Flamenco (No 242), Harlequin Green (No 298), Gorse (No 245), Crystal Rose (No 292) and Gay Turquoise (No 244). A pair of 5mm (No 6) knitting needles. Five buttons. Small amount of glass beads.

Measurements: To fit bust sizes up to 112cm (44") worn loosely.

Tension: 15 sts. measure about 10cm (4") with yarn used triple.

Abbreviations: k., knit; p., purl; st.(s.), stitch(es); st.st., stocking stitch; cont., continue; beg., beginning; rem., remain(ing); inc., increase; rep., repeat; dec., decrease; cm, centimetres; alt., alternate.

Metrication note: Apart from measurements above no reference to inches is made in pattern.

NB: All yarn is used triple throughout.

BACK

Using 5mm needles and main colour used triple, cast on 92 sts. and work 5cm in k.1, p.1 rib. Change to st.st. and work 36 rows. Now follow Back graph from 1st row and complete the 90 rows. Work straight until Back measures 75cm from beg.

Shape Shoulders: Cast off 9 sts. at beg. of the next 2 rows, and 8 sts. at beg. of next 6 rows. Cast off the rem. 26 sts. to give a firm neck edge.

Pocket linings (two Alike):

Using main, cast on 20 sts. and work 13cm in st.st. ending after a k. row. Leave sts. on a spare needle.

LEFT FRONT

Using main colour cast on 42 sts. and work 5cm in k.1, p.1 rib. Change to st.st. and work 10cm, ending after a k. row.

Next row: Work 11 sts. in st.st. (k.1, P.1) 10 times, work 11 sts. st.st Rep. this row 4 times more, thus ending after a wrong side row.

Next row: K.11 sts., cast off next 20 sts., K.11.

Next row: P.11, then p. across sts. of one pocket lining, p.11. Now working from 1st row, follow Left Front graph, shaping Front as shown. When graph is completed, cont. in st.st. in main colour until Front measures as Back to shoulder, ending at side edge.

Shape Shoulder:
Cast off 9 sts. at beg. of next row and 8 sts. on next 3 alt. rows.

RIGHT FRONT
Work to match Left Front until pocket is inserted, then work 15 rows straight in main colour. Now follow Right Front chart, thus beg. on a wrong side row. When graph is complete, cont. to match other front.

SLEEVES (Right Sleeve)
Using main colour cast on 42 sts. and work in k.1, p.1 rib for 5cm, inc. 1 st. at end of last row . . . 43 sts. Change to st.st., inc. 1 st. each end of every 5th row until there are 55 sts. Work 4 rows straight, thus ending after a p. row. Work from Back graph as given in dotted box in colours 1 and 3 (pink and green), thus small pink star will commence:
Next row: Inc in 1st st. k.20 navy, 1 pink, 11 navy, 1 pink, 20 navy, inc. in last st. Cont. to follow graph, but at same time still inc. at side edges as before until there are 71 sts. Cont. straight until sleeve measures 44cm (or length required). Cast off.

Left Sleeve
Work to match other sleeve but working colours 3 and 4 (green and yellow).

Left Front Band And Half Collar
Using main colour cast on 8 sts. and work in k.1, p.1 rib until band, very slightly stretched, reaches 1st front shaping, then on inner edge, inc. 1 st. on next 10 rows, then on every alt. row until there are 33 sts. Cont. straight until band is long enough to reach shoulder, ending at outer edge.

Shape For Back Collar:
Next 2 rows: Rib to last 8 sts., turn and rib back.
Next 2 Rows: Rib to last 16 sts., turn and rib back.
Next 2 rows: Rib to last 22 sts., turn and rib back.
Next 2 rows: Rib to last 28 sts., turn and rib back. Cont. straight in rib until collar reaches centre of back neck. Leave on spare needle.

Right Front Band And Half Collar:
First mark Left Front Band with pins as a guide for buttonholes, 1st pin 4 rows up from lower edge, 2nd pin 4 rows down from 1st front shaping and 3 more at equal distances between. Cast on 8 sts. and work in k.1, p.1 rib for 4 rows.
Next row (front edge): Rib 3, cast off 2, rib to end. In next row cast on 2 sts. in place of those cast off. Now work to match other band working buttonholes at pin positions. Cast off back neck sts. together.

TO MAKE UP
Press work according to ball band instructions. Join shoulders. Sew on bands and collar neatly. Using contrasting colours to background explosion colour, embroider in stem-stitch wavy lines as shown in photograph, then sew on beads beneath the exploding fireworks. Sew in sleeves, then sew up sleeve and side seams. Sew on buttons.

RIGHT FRONT

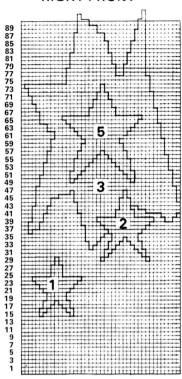

LEFT FRONT

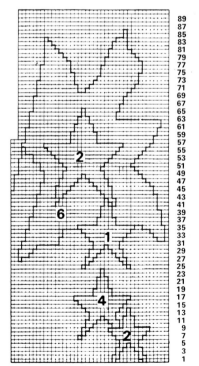

COLOUR KEY
1 = pink; 2 = red; 3 = green; 4 = yellow; 5 = peacock; 6 = royal. *Right sleeve:* large 2; small 1. *Left sleeve:* large 4; small 5. Dotted lines indicate pattern to be worked on sleeves.

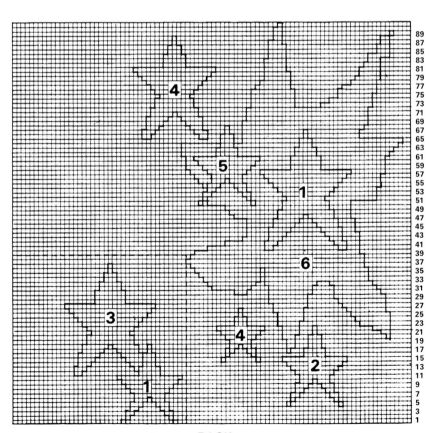

BACK

COTTON CABLE CARDIGAN

Materials: 13 (14, 15) 50g balls of Pingouin Coton Natural 8 fils. A pair of 3mm (No 11) and 4mm (No 8) knitting needles. A cable needle. Seven buttons. Lace collar.

Measurements: To fit a 81-86 (89-94, 97-102)cm – 32"-34" (35"-37", 38"-40"). Length from top of shoulders, 51 (52, 53)cm – 20" (20½", 21"). Sleeve seam, 42 (43, 44)cm – 16½" (17", 17½").

Tension: 12 sts. and 13 rows measures 5cm (2") over every slightly stretched pattern.

Abbreviations: k., knit; p., purl; st.(s). stitch(es); patt., pattern; rep., repeat; tog., together; sl., slip; cont., continue; alt., alternate; rem., remain(ing); beg., beginning; inc., increase; dec., decrease.

Size Note: Follow 1st figures for 1st size, 2nd figures for 2nd size and 3rd figures for 3rd size.

Metrication Note: Apart from measurements above no mention of inches is made in pattern.

BACK

Using 3mm needles cast on 99(103, 109) sts. and work 19 rows in k.1, p.1 rib.

Next row: Rib 5(7, 5) *inc. in next st., rib 10(7, 7). Rep. from * to last 6(8, 8) sts., inc. in next st., rib 5(7, 7). 108(115, 122) sts. Change to 4mm needles and work in patt. thus:

1st row: *p.3, k.4. Rep. from * to last 3 sts., p.3.

2nd row: *k.3, p.4. Rep. from * to last 3 sts., k.3.

3rd row: As 1st row.

4th row: As 2nd row.

5th row: *p.1, make a bobble in next st. thus: (k.1, p.1, k.1) all into next st., turn, p.3, turn, k.1, k.2 tog., sl. the k.1 over the k.2 tog. – this completes bobble, p.1, sl. next 2 sts. on cable needle and leave at front of work, k.2, then k.2 from cable needle. Rep. from * to last 3 sts., p.1, make a bobble in next st., p.1.

6th row: As 2nd row.

7th row: As 1st row.

8th row: As 2nd row.

These 8 rows form the patt. Cont. straight in patt. until Back measures 33(34, 35)cm from beg. ending after a wrong side row.

Shape Armholes:

Cast off 3(4, 5) sts. at beg. of next 2 rows, then k.2 tog. at each end of next and every alt. row until 80(87, 94) sts. rem. Work straight until Back measures 51(52, 53)cm from beg. ending after a wrong side row.

Shape Shoulders:

Cast off 7(8, 9) sts. at beg. of next 6 rows. Cast off rem. sts.

LEFT FRONT

Using 3mm needles cast on 53(59, 63) sts. and work 19 rows in k.1, p.1 rib.

Next row: Rib 6 and leave on safety pin for border, rib 5(6, 4), * inc. in next st., rib 8(7, 5). Rep. from * to last 6(7, 5) sts., inc. in next st., rib 5(6, 4). 52(59, 66) sts. Change to 4mm needles and cont. in patt. as for Back until Front measures 33(34, 35)cm from beg. ending with same row as Back to armholes.

Shape Armhole:

Cast off 3(4, 5) sts. at beg. of next row then dec. 1 st. at armhole edge on every alt. row until 38(45, 52) sts. rem. Work straight until Front measures 42(43, 44)cm, ending at neck edge.

Shape Neck:

Cast off 7(9, 11) sts. at beg. of next row, then k.2 tog. at this edge on next 4(6, 8) rows, then at this edge on next 6 alt. rows. 21(24, 27) sts. Work a few rows straight until Front measures same as Back to shoulder ending at armhole edge.

Shape Shoulder:

Cast off 7(8, 9) sts. at beg. of next and following 2 alt. rows.

RIGHT FRONT

Work as for Left Front for 2 rows.

Next row: Rib 3, cast off 2, rib to end. In next row cast on 2 sts. in place of those cast off. Work a further 14 rows in rib.

Next row: Rib to last 6 sts., turn and leave these 6 sts. on safety pin. Inc. across 47(53, 57) sts. on next row as for Left Front. Now work to match other front reversing all shapings.

SLEEVES

Using 3mm needles cast on 41 sts. for each size and work 8cm in k.1 p.1 rib, inc. across last row thus: rib 5, * inc. in next st., rib 2. Rep. from * to last 6 sts, inc. in next st., rib 5. 52 sts. Change to 4mm needles and work in patt. as for Back, inc. 1 st. each end of 9th(7th, 7th) row and every 6th row following until there are 78(80, 82) sts., working inc. sts. into patt. Cont. straight until sleeve measures 42(43, 44)cm from beg. or length required, ending after a wrong side row.

Shape Top:

Cast off 3(4, 5) sts. at beg. of next 2 rows, then dec. 1 st. each end of next and every alt. row until 52(50, 50) sts. rem., then each end of every row until 20(18, 18) sts. rem. Cast off.

FRONT BORDERS AND NECK-BAND

Do not press. Join shoulders.

Left Front Border. Go back to the 6 sts. on safety pin. Then with right side facing, join yarn to inside edge and using 3mm needles work in rib until border slightly stretched reaches to neck edge ending at inner edge. Leave on safety pin. Sew on border.

Right Front Border: Place pins in left front border as a guide for buttonholes, 1st pin 6cm from neck edge (7th buttonhole will be worked in centre of neck border). Place four more at equal distances between buttonhole in welt and 1st pin. Now work to match other border working buttonholes at pin positions and ending at outer edge. Sew on border.

Neck Border: Rib across the 6 sts. of right front border, pick up and k.26(28, 30) sts. up right front neck, 34(34, 36) sts. across back neck, 26(28, 30) sts. down left side of neck, then rib across the 6 sts. of left front border. Work 3 rows in k.1, p.1 rib, then work a 7th buttonhole in line with previous one in next 2 rows. Work 1 more row, then cast off in the rib.

TO MAKE UP

Join side and sleeve seams. Sew in sleeves. Sew on buttons to correspond with buttonholes. Press seams only on wrong side. Sew on bought lace collar beg. and ending in centre of front borders.

COOL COTTON JUMPER

Abbreviations: k., knit; p., purl; st(s)., stitch(es); st.st., stocking stitch; cm, centimetres; beg., beginning; dec., decrease; alt., alternate; rem., remain(ing); inc., increase; foll., following; sl., slip; psso., pass slip stitch over; tog., together; rep., repeat.

Size Note: Where 4 figures are given, follow 1st figures for 1st size, 2nd figures for 2nd size, 3rd figures for 3rd size and 4th figures for 4th size.

Metrication Note: except for above no mention of inches is made in pattern.

BACK AND FRONT ALIKE

Using 2¾mm needles and main shade No 21, cast on 106(110, 114, 118) sts. and work in k.2, p.2 rib for 8cm, inc. across last row thus: Inc. row: Rib 8(5, 6, 9) * inc. in next st., rib 10(10, 9, 8). Rep. from * ending inc. in next st., rib 9(5, 7, 9)...115(120, 125, 130) sts. Change to 3mm needles and work in st.st. until length is 36(37, 37, 38)cm from beg. ending after a p. row.

Shape raglan:
Cast off 3 sts. at beg. of next 2 rows, then dec. 1 st. each end of every alt. row to 95(100, 105, 110) sts., thus ending after a p. row. Leave sts. on spare needle.

SLEEVES

Using 2¾mm needles and main shade, cast on 82(82, 90, 90) sts. and work in k.2, p.2 rib for 5cm. Change to 3mm needles and work in st.st. inc. 1 st. each end of every foll. 6th row until there are 90(90, 100, 100) sts. Work straight until sleeve measures 17(18, 18, 19)cm from beg. ending after a p. row.

Shape raglan:
Cast off 3 sts. at beg. of next 2 rows, then dec. 1 st. at each end of every alt. row until 70(70, 80, 80) sts. rem. Leave on spare needle.

YOKE

Transfer all sts. to circular needle ... 330(340, 370, 380) sts. Mark the beg. of yoke with a coloured thread to denote beg. of every round, and when changing yarn also mark beg. of round. Now beg. at right side of Back and work in Fair Isle pattern from charts A, B and C, across Back, first sleeve, front, then second sleeve, and work dec. rounds as shown on charts.

These are as follows:
On 17th round of pink band, work * sl.1, k.1, psso., k.6, k.2 tog. Rep. from * all round ... 264(272, 296, 304) sts.
On 17th round of beige band, work * sl.1, k.1, psso., k.4, k.2 tog. Rep. from * all round ... 198(204, 222, 228) sts.
On 7th round of rust band, work * sl.1, k.1, psso., k.2, k.2 tog. Rep. from * all round ... 132(136, 148, 152) sts.
Now work 3(3, 6, 6) rounds in rust, then work k.2, p.2 rib for 8 rounds. Cast off in the rib.

TO MAKE UP

Fasten off all loose ends. Press work on wrong side (except rib) with a warm iron over a damp cloth. Join small raglan seams, then join sleeve and side seams. Press seams.

MATERIALS: Twilleys Stalite in main shade No 21 6(6, 7, 7,) balls and one ball of each of the contrast shades, No 9 (rust), No 30 (pink), No 27 (gold), No 37 (dark brown) and No 22 (beige). A pair of 2¾mm (old No 12) and 3mm (old No 11) knitting needles. A 3mm (old No 11) circular knitting needle.

MEASUREMENTS: To fit a 81(86, 91, 97)cm – 32"(34", 36", 38") bust.
Length 56(57, 58, 59)cm – 22"(22½", 22¾", 23¼").
Sleeve seam 17(18, 18, 19)cm – 6¾"(7", 7", 7½").

TENSION: 14 sts. and 18 rows measure 5cm (2") over plain st.st.

FRILLED ALPACA SWEATER

Materials: 9(9, 10) 50g balls Alpaca in Main (M.). 1 50g ball Alpaca in 3 contrast shades (C.). A pair of 3¾mm (old No 9) and 2¾mm (old No 12) knitting needles.

Measurements: To fit a 86(91, 97)cm – 34"(36", 38") bust – worn loosely.

Tension: 23 sts. measure about 10cm (4").

Abbreviations:

k., knit; p., purl; st.(s)., stitch(es); st.st., stocking stitch; cont., continue; alt., alternate; rep., repeat; foll., following; dec., decrease; inc., increase; rem., remain(ing); tog., together; beg., beginning; patt., pattern; g.st., garter stitch; tbl., through back of loop; yrn., yarn round needle; p.u.k., pick up loop before next st. and k. or p. into back of it; ch., chain; dc., double crochet; cm, centimetres; M., main; C., contrast; D., dark colour; L., light colour.

Size note: Follow 1st figures for 1st size and respective figures in brackets for larger sizes.

Metrication note: Except for materials, measurements and tension, no mention of inches is made in pattern.

BACK AND FRONT ALIKE

Using 2¾mm needles and M. cast on 107(113, 119) sts. and work in k.1, p.1 rib for 6cm. Change to 3¾mm needles and work in patt. thus;

1st row: K.5, * p.1, k.5. Rep. from * to end.

2nd row: K.1, * p.3, k.3. Rep. from * ending p.3, k.1.

3rd row: P.2, * k.1, p.5. Rep. from * ending k.1, p.2.

4th row: P.2, * k.1, p.5. Rep. from * ending k.1, p.2.

5th row: K.1, * p.3, k.3. Rep. from * ending p.3, k.1.

6th row: K.5, * p.1, k.5. Rep. from * to end. These 6 rows form the patt. Rep. them but on 2nd row of next patt. work thus:

8th row: Join on 1st C., k.1 C., * p.3 M., k.3 C. Rep. from * ending p.3 M., k.1.C. Cont. in patt. but on every 9th row, change to C. colours, using 2nd contrast

on all p. sts. in 17th row, 3rd C. on all k. sts. in 26th row, 1st C. on all p. sts. in 35th row, 2nd C. on all k. sts. in 44th row. Cont. thus until work measures 36(38, 40)cm.

Shape Armholes:

Cast off 9 sts. at beg. of next 2 rows, then cont. straight until work measures 51(53, 55)cm, ending after a wrong side row.

Shape Neck:

Next row: Patt. 37(40, 43) sts. and leave on spare needle, cast off next 15 sts., patt. to end. Now cast off 2 sts. at beg. of next neck edge row and every alt. row until 25(28, 31) sts. rem. Cont. straight until work measures 58(60, 62)cm.

Shape Shoulder:

Cast off 7(8, 9) sts. at beg. of next 2 armhole edge rows and 11(12, 13) sts. on next armhole edge row. Go back to sts. on spare needle, rejoin yarns and work to match first side.

SLEEVES (Alike)

Using 2¾mm needles and M. cast on 52 sts. for each size and work in k.1, p.1 rib for 6cm.

Next row: Rib 2, * p.u.k. rib 2. Rep. from * to end of row . . . 77 sts. Change to 3¾mm needles and work in patt. as for back and front, inc. 1 st. each end of every 6th row until there are 101 sts. for each size, working extra sts. into patt. Cont. straight until work measures 52cm – or length required. Cast off.

NECKBAND (All Alike)

Join right shoulder. Using 2¾mm needles and M., pick up and k.22 sts. down left front, 15 sts. across centre front, 22 sts. to right shoulder, 22 sts. down right back, 15 sts. across centre back neck and 22 sts. up left back . . . 118 sts. Work in k.1. p.1 rib for 10 rows. Cast off using the larger needle.

NECK FRILLS

Using 3¾mm needles and 1st C. cast on 13 sts. and work thus:

1st row: K.

2nd and 3rd rows: P.10, turn k.10.

4th row: P.10, k.3.

5th row: K.

6th and 7th rows: P.10, turn k.10.

8th row: P.10, k.3.

9th row: K.

10th row: K.

Break off C., join on M.

11th row: K.3, p.10.

12th and 13th rows: K.10, turn, p.10.

14th row: K.

15th row: K.3, p.10.

16th and 17th rows: K10, turn, p.10.

18th row: K.

19th row: K.3, p.10.

20th row: P.10, k.3.

Rep. these 20 rows 19 times more for Frill A, 23 times more using 2nd C. for Frill B and 29 times using 3rd C. for Frill C. Cast off.

TO MAKE UP

Do not press. Sew up left shoulder and neckband seam. Sew frill edges together to form circles. Now pin Frill A with C. colour uppermost to neck edge, about 6 rows down, with seam to shoulder edge, easing frill evenly. Sew in position. Then pin Frill B in place, so that it just tucks under Frill A and the join will not be visible. Stitch in place. Sew on Frill C in the same way (see photograph). Sew up side seam, then sew up sleeves leaving top 4cm open. Sew this open part to the cast off armhole sts., then sew in sleeve.

GILT-EDGED CARDIGAN

Materials: 20 balls Pengouin Sport 100% wool. 1 20g ball Place Vendôme in gold. A pair of 4mm (old No 8) and 5mm (old No 6) knitting needles. A medium size crochet hook. 5 buttons.

Measurements: To fit a 91cm (36") bust – worn loosely.

Tension: Approx. 17 sts. and 23 rows to 10cm (4").

Abbreviations:

k., knit; p., purl; st.(s)., stitch(es); st.st., stocking stitch; cont., continue; alt., alternate; rep., repeat; foll., following; dec., decrease; inc., increase; rem., remain(ing); tog., together; beg., beginning; patt., pattern; g.st., garter stitch; tbl., through back of loop; yrn., yarn round needle; p.u.k., pick up loop before next st. and k. or p. into back of it; ch., chain; dc., double crochet; cm, centimetres; M., main; C., contrast; D., dark colour; L., light colour.

Size note: Follow 1st figures for 1st size and respective figures in brackets for larger sizes.

Metrication note: Except for materials, measurements and tension, no mention of inches is made in pattern.

BACK.

Using 4mm needles and Sports wool, cast on 92 sts. and work in k.2, p.2 rib for 18 rows. Change to 5mm needles and work 95 rows in st.st. thus ending with a k. row.

Shape Armholes:

Cast off 4 sts. at beg. of next 2 rows, then dec. 1 st. each end of next 10 rows. Now work 35 rows straight, thus ending with a p. row. Leave sts. on spare needle.

RIGHT FRONT

Using 4mm needles and Sports wool cast on 46 sts. and work in k.2, p.2 rib for 18 rows. ** Change to 5mm needles and work 95 rows in st.st. thus ending after a k. row.

Shape Armhole:

Cast off 4 sts., p. to end of row.

Next row: K. Now dec. 1 st. at armhole edge on next 10 rows. Work 21 rows straight thus ending at front edge.

Shape Neck:

Cast off 6 sts., k. to end.

Next row: P. to neck edge. Now dec. 1 st. at neck edge on next 6 rows. Work 6 rows straight thus ending after a p. row. Leave sts. on spare needle.

LEFT FRONT

Work as right front to **. Change to 5mm needles and work 96 rows in st.st. thus ending after a p. row.

Shape Armhole:

Cast off 4 sts., k. to end. Now dec. 1 st. at armhole edge on next 10 rows. Work 22 rows straight, thus ending at front edge.

Shape Neck:

Cast off 6 sts., p. to end.

Next row: K. to neck edge. Now dec. 1 st. at neck edge on next 6 rows. Work 5 rows straight thus ending after a p. row. Leave sts. on spare needle.

SLEEVES

Using 4mm needles and Sports wool cast on 36 sts. and work in k.2, p.2 rib for 24 rows. Change to 5mm needles and work in st.st. inc. 1 st. each end of 1st and every 7th row until there are 62 sts., then work 5 rows straight (90 rows of st.st. worked).

Shape Top:

Cast off 4 sts. at beg. of next 2 rows, then dec. 1 st. each end of next 8 alt. rows, then each end of next 12 rows. Cast off rem. 14 sts.

Collar frill:

Using 4mm needles cast on 24 sts. and work 178 rows in st.st. Cast off.

Shoulder Frill:

Using 4mm needles cast on 26 sts and work 360 rows st.st. Cast off.

Right front band:

Using 4mm needles cast on 86 sts. and work 2 rows in st.st.

Next row: K.3, * cast off 3 sts., k.16 – including st. already on right-hand needle from casting off. Rep. from * 3 times more, cast off 3 sts., k. to end. In next row cast on 3 sts. in place of those cast off. Work 4 rows, then in next 2 rows work buttonholes as before. Work 2 more rows and cast off.

Left front band:

Using 4mm needles cast on 86 sts. and work in st.st. for 12 rows. Cast off.

TO MAKE UP

Graft or cast off shoulder sts. Press work as given on ball band. Sew in sleeves, then sew up sleeve and side seams. Sew on bands, then fold in half to wrong side and slipstitch down. Buttonhole stitch round buttonholes. Fold collar in half, right sides facing and stitch short side seams. Turn to right side. Gather one long edge to fit neck, and sew on, beg. and ending at centre of band. Gather other edge to match and stitch in position. Measure down 13cm from neck, mark yoke line with coloured thread beg. and ending inside front bands. Gather frill at one long edge to fit and neatly sew in place, sewing down the short ends inside band edges. Now using crochet hook and gold fingering work in d.c. along folded edge of collar and free long edge of yoke frill. Mark a graph with coloured thread as a guide then using gold fingering work in ch.st. to form trellis patt. (see photograph). Sew on buttons. Turn back cuffs.

JACK OF HEARTS PULLOVER

Materials: Of Sirdar Majestic Double Knitting, 50g balls, 5(5, 6) balls in Ivory, 2(2, 2) balls in Festive Scarlet, and 1(1, 1) ball in each of Banana and Black. A pair of 4mm (old No 8) and 3¼mm (old No 10) knitting needles.

Measurements: To fit a 97(102, 107)cm – 38"(40", 42") chest. Length: 63 (66,69)cm – 25"(26", 27")

Tension: 22 sts. and 28 rows measure 10cm (4") over st.st.

Abbreviations:

k., knit; p., purl; st.(s.), stitch(es); st.st., stocking stitch; cont., continue; alt., alternate; rep., repeat; foll., following; dec., decrease; inc., increase; rem., remain(ing); tog., together; beg., beginning; patt., pattern; g.st., garter stitch; tbl., through back of loop; yrn., yarn round needle; p.u.k., pick up loop before next st. and k. or p. into back of it; ch., chain; dc., double crochet; cm, centimetres; M., main; C., contrast; D., dark colour; L., light colour.

Size note: Follow 1st figures for 1st size and respective figures in brackets for larger sizes.

Metrication note: Except for materials, measurements and tension, no mention of inches is made in pattern.

BACK

Using 3¼mm needles and Ivory cast on 113(119, 125) sts. and work 14 rows in k.1, p.1 rib inc. 1 st. at end of last row . . . 114(120, 126) sts. Change to 4mm needles and cont. in st.st. for 2(10, 18) rows.

Next row: K.23(26, 29) Ivory, 68 Scarlet, 23(26, 29) Ivory.

Next row: P.23(26, 29) Ivory, 68 Scarlet, 23(26, 29) Ivory.

Next row: K.23(26, 29) Ivory, 2 Scarlet, then rep. the 8 sts. of back graph (see page 84) for 1st row, 8 times, 2 Scarlet, 23(26, 29) Ivory.

Next row: P.23(26, 29) Ivory, 2 Scarlet, rep. the 8 sts. of 2nd row of back graph 8 times, 2 Scarlet, 23(26, 29) Ivory. Cont. working graph in this way, keeping 2 sts. each end of Fair Isle patt. in Scarlet until 12 reps. of patt. have been completed . . . 100(108, 116) rows of st.st. worked.

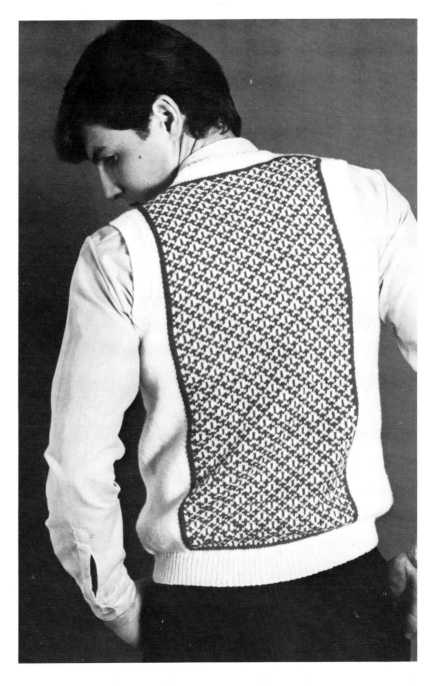

Shape Armholes:
Cast off 9(10, 11) sts. at beg. of next 2 rows, then dec. 1 st. at beg. of next and every foll. row until 78(80, 82) sts. rem. Cont. straight until 19 rep. of patt, have been worked from beg., then work the 4 rows of next patt.
Next row: K.5(6, 7) Ivory, 68 Scarlet, 5(6, 7) Ivory.
Next row: P.5(6, 7) Ivory, 68 Scarlet, 5(6, 7) Ivory. Work 2 rows Ivory in st.st.
Shape Shoulders:
Cast off 20(21, 22) sts. at beg. of next 2 rows. Cast off rem. 38 sts.
FRONT
Work as for back to **
Next row: K.23(26, 29) Ivory, work 1st row of Front graph (to avoid stranding use a separate ball of wool for each colour change, but remembering to strand yarn at change over to avoid a hole) k.23(26, 29) Ivory.
Next row: P.23(26, 29) Ivory, work 2nd row of graph, p.23(26, 29) Ivory. Cont. working from graph in this way until the 81st row (a k. row) has been worked. Then work from base upwards for 17 rows (same number of rows to armhole as on Back).
Shape Armholes:
Cast off 9(10, 11) sts. at beg. of next 2 rows, then dec. 1 st. at beg. of next and every foll. row until 78(80, 82) sts. rem. Cont. straight for 17 rows (Jack's face design on chart now reached). Work the next 3 rows from graph but working over centre face design in Ivory only (see photograph).
Shape Neck:
Next row: K.27 (28, 29), turn and leave rem. sts. on spare needle. Now dec. 1 st. at beg of next and every foll. alt. row at neck edge until 20(21, 22) sts, rem. Cont. straight until graph is completed. Work 1 row in Ivory and cast off. Go back to other sts., rejoin yarn, cast off centre 24 sts.,

then following graph work across rem. 27(28, 29) sts.
Next row: Work to end. Now work to correspond with other side.
NECKBAND (All alike)
Join left shoulder seam. Now using 3¼ mm needle Ivory and right side of work facing, pick up and k.38 sts. from back neck, 18 sts. down left front, 24 sts., from centre and 19 sts. up right front . . . 99 sts. Work 8 rows in k.1, p.1 rib. Cast off loosely in rib. Join right shoulder and neckband seam.
ARMBANDS
Using 3¼mm needles and Ivory and with right side of work facing, pick up and k.117(119, 121) sts. evenly all round armholes and work 8 rows in k.1, p.1 rib. Cast off loosely in rib.
TO MAKE UP
Sew in ends. Press, working from ball band instructions. Join side and armband seams. Press seams.

81st row

Back graph

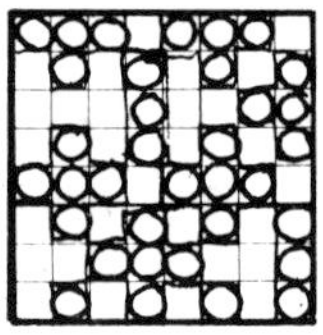

Start here

Front graph ▶

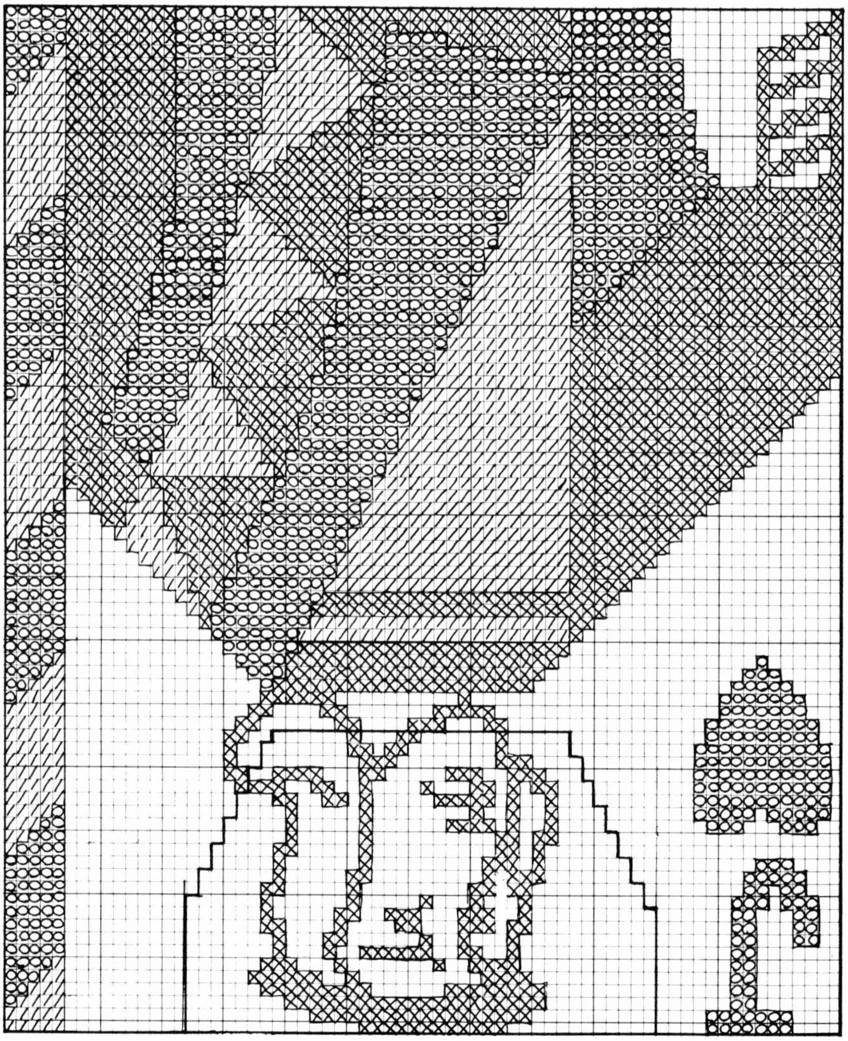

Start here

MOHAIR KIMONO AND SLIPOVER

Materials: 13(13, 14) 25g balls of Hayfield Gossamer in Grey (L.), 10 balls in Black (D.) and 3 balls in Pink. A pair of 5mm (old No 6) and 5½mm (old No 5) knitting needles. Small amount of white Gossamer for embroidery.

Measurements: To fit a 86(91, 97)cm – 34"(36",38") bust. Length from back neck, 81cm (32"). Sleeve length: 44cm (17½") adjustable.

Tension: 8 sts. measures 5cm (2").

Abbreviations:

k., knit; p., purl; st.(s.), stitch(es); st.st., stocking stitch; cont., continue; alt., alternate; rep., repeat; foll., following; dec., decrease; inc., increase; rem., remain(ing); tog., together; beg., beginning; patt., pattern; g.st., garter stitch; tbl., through back of loop; yrn., yarn round needle; p.u.k., pick up loop before next st. and k. or p. into back of it; ch., chain; dc., double crochet; cm, centimetres; M., main; C., contrast; D., dark colour; L., light colour.

Size note: Follow 1st figures for 1st size and respective figures in brackets for larger sizes.

Metrication note: Except for materials, measurements and tension, no mention of inches is made in pattern.

BACK

Using 5mm needles and D. cast on 86(88, 92) sts. and work 8 rows in g.st. Change to 5½mm needles and joining in L. as required work in st.st. patt. thus:

1st row: K.7(8, 10) L., * 2 D., 2 L., 2 D., 16 L. Rep. from * twice more, k.2 D., 2 L., 2 D., 7(8, 10) L.

2nd row: As 1st row but p. instead of k.

3rd to 20th rows: Rep. last 2 rows 9 times more.

21st row: K. to end in D.

22nd row: P. to end in D.

23rd and 24th rows: As 1st and 2nd rows.

25th and 26th rows: As 21st and 22nd rows.

These 26 rows form the patt. Cont. straight until work measures about 78cm from beg. ending after the 10th row of the 6th square.

Shape Shoulders:
Cast off 8 sts. at beg. of next 4 rows, 8(9, 10) sts. at beg. of next 2 rows. Cast off rem. 38(38, 40) sts.

LEFT FRONT
Using 5mm needles and D., cast on 49(50, 52) sts. and work 8 rows in g.st. Change to 5½mm needles and set patt. thus:

1st row: K.7(8, 10) L., 2 D., 2 L., 2 D., 16 L., 2 D., 2 L., 2 D., 8 L, slip rem. 6 sts. on to safety pin for left front band. Cont. in patt. as set to match back until the 13th row of 4th square has been worked.

Shape front:
Dec. 1 st. at front edge on the next and every foll. alt. row until 24(25, 26) sts. rem. Cont. straight until front measures same as back to shoulder, ending at side edge.

Shape Shoulder:
Cast off 8 sts. at beg. of next and foll. alt, rows. Work 1 row, then cast off 8(9, 10) sts.

RIGHT FRONT
Work to match left front reversing all shapings' and set patt. thus: Leave the first 6 sts. on a safety pin for border, k.8 L., 2 D., 2 L., 2 D., 16 L., 2 D., 2 L., 2 D., 7(8, 10) L.

SLEEVES
Using 5mm needles and D. cast on 46 (48, 50) sts. and work in g. st. for 8 rows. Change to 5½mm needles and patt. as follows:

1st row: K.9(10, 11) L., 2 D., 2 L., 2 D., 16 L., 2 D., 2 L., 2 D., 9(10, 11) L. (Read next paragraph through before commencing.)

Cont. in patt. as set, but for the first square beg. from row 15(13, 11) to row 26, then rep. from 1st to 26th row. However, if a longer sleeve is required work the extra rows at lower edge – not at

top of sleeve. *At the same time* inc. 1 st. each end of every 3rd row to 94(96, 98) sts. working the extra sts. into patt. Work straight until the 12th (10th, 8 th) row of the 4th square from beg. has been worked. Cast off.

Left front band:
Join shoulders. Slip the 6 sts. from pin on to a 5mm needle with right side of work facing. Work in g.st. using D. until band is long enough, very slightly stretched, to fit up front edge and to centre back neck. Leave sts. on a spare needle.

Right front band:
Work as for left front band.

TO MAKE UP
Graft front bands at centre back neck. Sew front bands in position. Sew in sleeves, then sew up side and sleeve seams. Now following chart and instructions work embroidery.

SASH
Using 5½mm needles and Pink, cast on 8 sts, and work in k.2 p.2 rib. Cont in rib, inc. 1 st. each end of every foll. 10th row until there are 20 sts. Work straight for 137cm (or longer if required, for sash to wrap twice around hips allowing for the extra rows worked for decreasing). Now dec. 1 st. each end of next and foll. 10th rows until 8 sts. rem. Cast off.

SLIPOVER

Materials: 7(7, 8) 25g balls of Hayfield Gossamer in Black. 5(6, 6) 25g balls of Hayfield Gossamer in White. A pair of 4½mm (old No 7) and 6mm (old No 4) knitting needles.

Measurements: To fit a 86(91, 97)cm – 34"(36", 38") bust. Length from shoulder, 56 (56.5, 57)cm – 22"(22¼", 22½")

TENSION: 8 sts. to 5cm (2").

Abbreviations, sizes and metrication note. See page 80.

BACK
** Using 4½mm needles and D., cast on 71(75, 79) sts. and work in k.1, p.1 rib for 3 rows. Join in L. and k.1 row, then work 1 row of rib. Change to D. and k.1 row, then work 3 rows of rib. Change to L. and k.1 row, then work 1 row of rib. Rep. the last 6 rows twice more. Change to D. and k.1 row, then work 1 row of rib inc. across row thus:

Inc. row: Rib 6(8, 10) p.u.k. (rib 6, p.u.k.) 10 times, rib 5(7, 9) . . . 82(86, 90) sts. Change to 6mm needles and work in check patt. thus:

1st row: * K.2 D., 2 L. Rep. from, * to last 2 sts., 2 D.

2nd row: As 1st row but p. instead of k.

3rd row: * K.2 L., 2 D. Rep. from * to last 2 sts., 2 L.

4th row: As 3rd row but p. instead of k. These 4 rows form the patt. Cont. in patt. until work measures 35.5cm from beg. ending with a p. row. Place a coloured thread at each end of row **

Work straight until back measures 56(56.5, 57)cm from beg. ending after a wrong side row.

Shape Shoulders:
Cast off 12 sts. at beg. of next 2 rows and 10(11, 12) sts. at beg. of next 2 rows. Leave rem. 38(40,42) sts. on a holder.

FRONT
Work as given for Back from ** to **

Shape Neck:
Next row: Patt. 41 (43, 45) sts., turn and leave rem. sts. on spare needle.

*** Dec. 1 st. at neck edge on the next and

foll. 10(11, 12) alt. rows, then dec. 1 st. at neck edge on next 8 rows . . . 22(23, 24) sts. rem. Cont. straight until work measures as back to shoulder, ending at side edge.

Shape Shoulder:
Cast off 12 sts. at beg. of next row, then cast off 10(11, 12) sts. on next alt. row. Go back to sts., on spare needle. Join yarn to next st. (centre) and work to end of row. Now work to match other side from ***

TO MAKE UP
Do not press. Join shoulders.

Neckband: With right side of work facing, using 4½mm needles and D., pick up and k.48(50, 52) sts. up right front edge to shoulder then k.19(20, 21) sts. from holder at back neck, turn. Work 1 row in k.1, p.1 rib. Change to L. and k.1 row, then work 1 row in rib. Change to D. and k.1 row then work 3 rows of rib. Change to L. and k.1 row, then work 1 row of rib. Change to D. and k.1 row, then work 1 row of rib, Cast off in rib. Go back to centre back neck. K. rem. sts. from holder, then pick up and k.48(50, 52) sts. down left side to centre front. Work in rib as for first side.

Armbands: With right side of work facing, using 4½mm needles and D. pick up and k.88(92, 96) sts. between markers at side edge. Work in rib as given for neckband. Join neckband at centre back. Cross left side neckband over right side and stitch down neckband at centre front. Sew up side and armband seams.

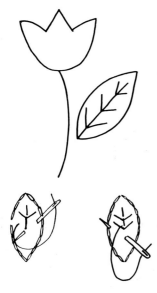

METHOD FOR EMBROIDERY
Sew up jacket. Using thin paper cut out 10 tulip shapes and 22 leaf shapes. (**NB** Diagrams given are approximately a quarter of the required size.) Position shapes on to jacket and pin in place. Sew around shapes using a chain stitch. Remove paper pieces and sew fly stitches inside each of the leaves. Sew a line of chain stitches for each of the stems.

PAISLEY SKIRT AND TOP

SKIRT

Materials for skirt: 22 balls 50g balls of Hayfield Brig DK, 22 balls in French Beige, 1 ball in Aqua, Cactus and Rustic Brick.

Sweater: 6(7, 7) balls in French Beige, 1 ball in Aqua and small amount of Rustic Brick. A pair of 4mm (old No 8) and 3¼ mm (old No 10) knitting needles. Elastic for skirt waist, about 2.5cm (1") wide.

Measurements for skirt: To fit 91(97, 102)cm 36"(38", 40") hips – adjust elastic to fit waist. Length 58cm (23"). **Note:** This length does not include the waistband and owing to the weight of the skirt, will drop slightly.

Sweater: To fit a 84(91, 97)cm – 34"(36", 38") bust.

TENSION: 6 sts. and 8 rows to 2.5cm (1") over st.st.

Abbreviations:

k., knit; p., purl; st.(s)., stitch(es); st.st., stocking stitch; cont., continue; alt., alternate; rep., repeat; foll., following; dec., decrease; inc., increase; rem., remain(ing); tog., together; beg., beginning; patt., pattern; g.st., garter stitch; tbl., through back of loop; yrn., yarn round needle; p.u.k., pick up loop before next st. and k. or p. into back of it; ch., chain; dc., double crochet; cm, centimetres; M., main; C., contrast; D., dark colour; L., light colour.

Size note: Follow 1st figures for 1st size and respective figures in brackets for larger sizes.

Metrication note: Except for materials, measurements and tension, no mention of inches is made in pattern.

SKIRT (worked in 6 panels)

Using 4mm needles and Aqua cast on 120 sts. and work thus:

1st row: * K.1, p.1. Rep. from * to end.
2nd row: As 1st row.
3rd row: * P.1, k.1. Rep. from * to end.
4th row: As 3rd row.
5th row: As 1st row.
6th row: As 1st row.

Break off Aqua and join on French Beige and cont. in st.st. for 7.5cm. Change to Aqua and work 4 rows in st.st. Change to French Beige and cont. in st.st. until work measures 58cm – or length required – ending after a p. row.
Next row: K.2 tog. to end of row (60 sts.).
Next row: P.2 tog. to end of row (30 sts.).
Cont. in st.st. for 6cm. cast off.

TO MAKE UP

Join panels together neatly. Turn over waistband and hem down leaving a small opening to insert elastic. Thread elastic through and close opening. Press lightly with a steam iron over a damp cloth. Embroider paisley design, enlarge diagram and make a stencil cut from paper or card, using a selection of satin stitch, chain and lazy daisy stitch and couching in Cactus, Rustic Brick and Aqua. Embroider star stripes in cross-stitch held together in centre, using Rustic Brick.

TOP

Note: The moss stitch trim on front part of sweater is picked up when front is completed and worked downwards.

BACK

Using Aqua and 4mm needles cast on 74(80, 86) sts. and work thus:
1st row: * K.1, p.1. Rep. from * to end.
2nd row: As 1st row.
3rd row: * P.1, k.1. Rep. from * to end.
4th row: As 3rd row.
5th and 6th rows: As 1st and 2nd rows.
** Change to French Beige and cont. in st.st. inc. 1 st. at each end of next and every foll. 4th row until there are 108(114, 120) sts. Cont. straight until work measures 25(27, 28)cm. or length required.

Shape Armholes:

Cast off 12(14, 16) sts. at beg. of next 2 rows, then dec. 1 st. at each end of next and every alt. row until 60(64, 68) sts. rem. Cont. straight until work measures 40.5(42, 43)cm. Cast off.

FRONT

Using French Beige and 4mm needles cast on 2 sts. Now working in st.st. inc. in each st. on first row then each end of every row until there are 20 sts., then p. next row. Now cast on 27(30, 33) sts. at beg. of next 2 rows . . . 74(80, 86) sts. Work as for back from ** until work measures 23.5(24.5, 26)cm (allowing for the trim to be added).

Shape Armholes:

Work as for back armholes, then cont. straight until work measures 32(33,34)cm ending after a p. row.

Shape Neck:

Next row: K.21 (23, 25), cast off 18 sts., k. to end. Cont. on last sts. only dec. 1 st. at neck edge of next 2 rows, then cont. straight until front measures 39(40, 41)cm. Cast off. Go back to remaining sts., rejoin yarn to other sts. and work to match first side.

Front Trim

Left Point: With right side of work facing, 4mm needles using Aqua, beg. from point and pick up and k.38 sts. to side.
Next row: P. Cont. thus:
1st row: (K.1, p.1) into same st., * k.1, p.1. Rep. from * ending p.1.
2nd row: * P.1, k.1. Rep. from * to last st (p.1, k.1) into same st.
3rd row: (P.1, k.1) into same st., * p.1, k.1. Rep. from * ending p.1.
4th row: * K.1, p.1. Rep. from * to last st. (k.1, p.1) into st.
5th row: * P.1, k.1. Rep. from * to end. Cast off.
Right Point: Using Aqua and with right side facing, beg. at side edge and pick up and k.38 sts. using 4mm needles. P. next row. Work thus:
1st row: * K.1, p.1. Rep. from * to last st., then (p.1, k.1) into st. Cont. in double moss st. to match other point, inc. 1 st. at point on next 3 rows.

SLEEVES

Using French Beige and 3¼mm needles cast on 72(76, 80) sts.
Next row: * K.1 tb1, p.1. Rep. from * to end. Cont. in twisted rib until cuff measures 6cm. Change to 4mm needles and work in st.st. inc. 1 st. at each end of next and every foll. alt. row until there are 112(116, 120) sts. Cont. in st.st. until work measures 20cm – or length required, ending after a p. row.

Shape Top:

Cast off 12(14, 14) sts. at beg. of next 2 rows, then dec. 1 st. at each end of next and every foll. 3rd row until 60(62, 62) sts. rem. Now dec. 1 st. at each end of every row until 40(42, 42) sts. rem. Cast off 6 sts. at beg. of next 4 rows. Cast off rem. sts.

COLLAR (2 Pieces Alike)

First join shoulders. Then with right side of work facing, and using 3¼mm needles and French Beige, beg. at centre front and pick up and k.50 sts. to shoulder and to centre back neck. Work 4cm in twisted k.1, p.1 rib, then change to Aqua and work 3 rows in double moss st. Cast off in moss st.
Work other side to match, but beginning from centre back neck.

TO MAKE UP

Press or steam garment. Join side seams. Sew up sleeve seams, then sew in sleeves, gathering sleeve top to fit. Sew point edges tog. Using Rustic Brick, embroider the star shapes, using cross-stitch held together in centre.

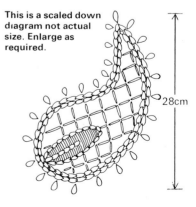

This is a scaled down diagram not actual size. Enlarge as required.

28cm

DEFTLY TEXTURED SWEATER

Materials: 11 50g balls Hayfield Falkland wool. A pair of 3¼mm (Old No 10) and 4mm (Old No 8) knitting needles. A set of 3¼mm (Old No 10) knitting needles with points each end.

Measurements: To fit a 87-91(97-102)cm – 34"-36" (38"-40") bust (worn loosely).

Tension: 6 sts. measures 2.5cm (1") over st.st. using 4mm (Old No 8) needles. If your tension is correct across st.st., it will be correct across the pattern.

> **Abbreviations:** k., knit; p., purl; st.(s.), stitch(es); tog., together; sl., slip; cont., continue; rep., repeat; patt., pattern; rem., remain; d.mst., double moss stitch; inc., increase.

Size Note: Follow 1st figures for 1st size and figures in brackets for 2nd size.

Metrication Note: Apart from measurements above, no reference to inches is made in pattern.

BACK

Using 3¼mm needles cast on 102 sts. for either size and work thus:

1st row: k.2, * p.2, k.2. Rep. from * to end (wrong side).

2nd row: p.2, * k.2, p.2. Rep. from * to end.

3rd row: As 1st row.

4th row: p.2, * k.2 tog., but leave on needle, then k. into front of 1st st. again and slip both sts. off needle, p.2. Rep. from * to end. Rep. these 4 rows 5 times more, then 1st row once more. Change to 4mm needles and inc. across row thus:

Next row (right side): k.5(0) then k. twice into next st., * k.4(3), k. twice into next st. Rep. from * ending k.1 ... 122(128) sts.

Next 5 rows: p.

**Work in d.mst. thus:

1st row (right side): * k.1, p.1. Rep. from * to end.

2nd row: As 1st row.

3rd and 4th rows: * p.1, k.1. Rep. from * to end.

Rep. 1st to 4th rows, 3 times more, then 1st to 3rd rows once more.

Next row: p. to end, inc. in 1st st. ... 123(129) sts.

Next 3 rows: p.

Work lattice patt. thus:

1st row (wrong side): p.

2nd row: k.2, * yarn to front, sl. next 5 sts., yarn back, k.1. Rep. from * to last st., k.1.

3rd row: p.

4th row: k.4, * insert needle under loose strand and k. next st. bringing st. out under strand, k.5. Rep. from * ending last repeat k.4 instead of k.5.

5th row: p.

6th row: k.1, yarn to front, sl. next 3 sts., yarn back, * k.1, yarn to front, sl. 5, yarn back. Rep. from * to last 5 sts., k.1, yarn to front, sl. 3, yarn back, k.1.

7th row: p.

8th row: k.1, * k. next st. under loose strand, k.5. Rep. from * ending last rep. k.1, instead of k.5. Rep. last 8 rows twice more.

Next 4 rows: k.

Next row: p.2 tog., p. to end ... 122(128) sts. ** Rep. from ** to ** once more, *** then cont. in d.mst. for 20cm. Cast off.

FRONT

Work as for Back to ***, then cont. in d.mst. for 13cm, ending after a wrong side row.

Shape Neck:

Next row: Work 42(45) sts. d.mst., cast off next 38 sts., d.mst. 42(45). Cont. on the last 42(45) sts. until work measures as Back. Cast off. Go back to rem. 42(45) sts., rejoin yarn and work to match first side.

SLEEVES

Using 3¼mm needles cast on 50 sts. for either size and work welt patt. as for Back for 17 rows, thus ending after a wrong side row. Change to 4mm needles.

Next row: * k.3, inc. in next st. Rep. from * ending k.2 (62 sts.).

Next 5 rows: p.

Now cont. in the 4 rows of d.mst., inc. 1 st. each end of every 5th row until there are 90 sts. working extra sts. into patt. Cont. straight until work measures 46cm from beginning or length required. Cast off.

COLLAR

Join shoulders. Then using the double pointed needles and beginning at centre front, pick up and k.104 sts. evenly round neck. Cont. in rounds thus:

1st round: * k.2, p.2. Rep. from * all round.

2nd and 3rd rounds: as 1st round.

4th round: * twist 2 sts. tog. (as in 4th row of Back welt), p.2. Rep. from * all round. Rep. these 4 rounds 3 times more.

Next row: * k.2, p.2. Rep. from * to end of round (centre front), turn.

Next row: * twist 2 tog., p.2. Rep. from * to end.

Next 2 rows: * k.2, p.2. Rep. from * to end. These last 4 rows will now have reversed the right and wrong side of the collar to allow for the collar to fold over. Rep. the last 4 rows 5 times more. Cast off.

TO MAKE UP

Press lightly over a damp cloth. Match centre of sleeve top to shoulder seam, and sew in sleeves. Sew up side and underarm seams.

ARAN SAMPLER SWEATER

Materials: 12(13, 14) 50g balls Robin Seascape. A pair of 4mm (Old No 8) and 5mm (Old No 6) knitting needles. A cable needle.

Measurements: To fit an 86(91, 97) cm, 34"(36", 38") bust. Length from shoulder, 64(65, 66) cm – 25"(25½", 26"). Sleeve seam, 46cm (18").

Tension: Approx 20 sts. and 24 rows measure 10cm (4") over different patterns, but not cable patt., using 5mm needles.

Abbreviations: k., knit; p., purl; st.(s.), stitch(es); st.st., stocking stitch; patt., pattern; rep., repeat; cont., continue; rem., remain(ing); alt., alternate; foll., following; inc., increase; dec., decrease; cm, centimentres; CF., cable front, ie slip next 2 sts. on to cable needle and leave at front, k. next 2 sts., then k.2 sts. from cable needle; CB – cable back, ie as CF but leave cable needle at back of work.

Size Note: Where 3 figures are given, follow 1st figures for 1st size, 2nd figures for 2nd size and 3rd figures for 3rd size.

Metrication Note: Apart from measurements above, no reference to inches is made in pattern.

BACK

Using 4mm needles cast on 92(100, 104) sts. and work in k.2, p.2 rib for 10cm, inc. 1 st. at each end of last row for 1st and 3rd sizes only . . . 94(100, 106) sts. Change to 5mm needles and work in patt. thus:

1st row: P.1(4, 7), * k.4, p.4. Rep. from * 5 times more, then k.1, p.3 11(11, 12) times, k.1, p.0(3, 2).

2nd row: P.1(0, 0), k.3(3, 2), * p.1, k.3. Rep. from * 9(10, 11) times more p.1, then k.4, p.4, 6 times, k.1(4, 7).

3rd and 4th rows: As 1st and 2nd rows.

5th row: P.1(4, 7) * CF, p.4. Rep. from * 5 times more, then k.1, p.3, 11(11, 12) times, k.1, p.0(3, 2).

6th row: As 2nd row.

7th and 8th rows: As 1st and 2nd rows.

9th-24th rows: Work 1st to 8th rows, twice more.

25th-30th rows: Work 1st to 6th rows once.

31st row: P.1(4, 7) * k.4, p.4. Rep. from * 5 times more, then p.4, k.4 3 times, p.5, then k.2, p.2, 4(4, 5) times, ending 2nd size k.2, p.1 and 3rd size k.2.

32nd row: *2nd size:* K.1, p.2, for 3rd size, p.2, then for all sizes cont. thus: k.2, p.2, 4(4, 5) times, k.5, then p.4, k.4, 3 times and k.4, p.4, 6 times, k.1(4, 7).

33rd and 34th rows: As 31st and 32nd rows.

35th row: P.1(4, 7) * k.4, p.4. Rep. from * 8 times more, k.4, p.1, then rib to end as before.

36th row: Rib 16(19, 22) as before, k.1, * p.4, k.4. Rep. from * 8 times more, p.4, k.1(4, 7).

37th row: P.1(4, 7) * CF, p.4. Rep. from * 5 times more, then k.4, p.4, 3 times, k.4, p.1, rib to end as before.

38th row: As 36th row.

39th-54th rows: Work 31st to 38th rows twice.

55th-58th rows: Work 31st to 34th rows once.

59th row: K.17(20, 23) p.1, then k.1, p.3, 5 times, k.39, p.1 then rib to end.

60th row: Rib 16(19, 22), k.1, p.39, now k.3, p.1 5 times, k.1, p.17(20, 23).

61st row: As 59th row.

62nd row: Rib 16(19, 22), k.1, p.39, then k.3, p.1, 5 times, k.18(21, 24).

63rd row: As 59th row.

64th row: Rib 16(19, 22), k.41, then p.1, k.3, 5 times, k.17(20, 23).

65th row: K.17(20, 23) then p.3, k.1, 5 times, p.1, k.39, p.1, rib to end.

66th and 67th rows: As 64th and 65th rows.

68th row: Rib 16(19, 22), k.41 then p.1, k.3, 5 times, p.17(20, 23)

69th-78th rows: As 59th to 68th rows.

79th and 80th rows: As 59th and 60th rows.

81st and 82nd rows: Work as 61st and 62nd rows but cast off 12 sts. at beg. of each row.

83rd-88th rows: As 63rd to 68th row but allowing for cast off armhole sts.

89th row: K.5(8, 11), p.1, then k.2, p.2, 5 times, now k.4, p.4, 5 times, k.4, p.0(3, 6).

90th row: K.0(3, 6), then p.4, k.4, 5 times, p.4, now k.2, p.2, 5 times, k.1, p.5(8, 11).

91st row: As 89th row.

92nd row: As 90th row but ending k.6(9, 12).

93rd row: K.5(8, 11), p.1, then k.2, p.2, 5 times, now CB, p.4, 5 times, CB, p.0(3, 6).

94th row: As 92nd row.

95th row: As 89th row.

96th row: As 92nd row.

97th and 98th rows: As 89th and 90th rows.

99th-118th row: Work last 10 rows twice more.

119th-124th row: Work from 91st-96th rows.

Cast off for 1st size but work 2(3) rows more for 2nd and 3rd sizes. Cast off.

Front

Work as for back until front measures 53cm ending after a wrong side row.

Shape Neck:

Next row: Patt. 30(32, 34) sts., turn. **

Next row: Cast off 3 sts., patt. to end. Now dec. 1 st. at neck edge on next 3 rows and foll. 2 alt. rows. Cont. straight on rem. 22(24, 26) sts. until front measures as back. Cast off. Go back to other sts. and with right side of work facing, leave centre 10(12, 14) sts. on spare needle, rejoin yarn to rem. 30(32, 34) sts. and work as for other side from **

SLEEVES

Using 4mm needles cast on 44(44, 48) sts. and work in k.2, p.2 rib for 7.5cm, inc. 1 st. at each end of last row for 2nd size only . . . 44(46, 48) sts. Change to 5mm needles and work in patt. thus:

1st row (right side): P.0(1, 2) then k.4, p.4, 3 times and k.1, p.3, 5 times, then end 2nd and 3rd sizes, k.1, p.0(1, 1).

2nd row: K.0(0, 1), p.0(1, 1) then k.3, p.1, 5 times, and k.4, p.4, 3 times, k.0(1, 2).

3rd and 4th rows: As 1st and 2nd rows.

5th row: P.0(1, 2), then CF, p.4, 3 times and k.1, p.3, 5 times ending 2nd and 3rd sizes as 1st row.

6th row: As 2nd row.

7th row: As 1st row but inc. 1 st. each end of row.

8th row: K.0(1, 2), p.1, then k.3, p.1, 5 times, and k.4, p.4, 3 times, k.1(2, 3).

9th-32nd row: Rep. 1st to 8th rows 3 times, inc. 1 st. at each end of 13th, 19th, 25th and 31st rows and working increased sts. on left side of sleeve in patt., and on right side of sleeve in reversed st.st. . . . 54(56, 58) sts.

33rd row: P.5(6, 7), then k.4, p.4, 3 times and p.4, k.4, 3 times, p.1(2, 3).

34th row: K.1 (2, 3), then p.4, k.4, 3 times and k.4, p.4, 3 times, k.5(6, 7).

35th and 36th rows: As 33rd and 34th rows.

37th row: Inc. in 1st st., p.4(5, 6), then CF, p.4, 3 times, and k.4, p.4 3 times, p.0(1, 2), inc. in last st.

38th row: k.2(3, 4) then k.4, p.4, 6 times, k.6(7, 8).

39th row: p.6(7, 8) then k.4, p.4, 6 times, p.2(3, 4).

40th row: As 38th row.

41st-56th rows: Rep. 33rd to 40th rows twice, inc. 1 st. at each end of 43rd, 49th and 55th row and working increased edges as before . . . 62(64, 66) sts.

57th row: P.9(10, 11) then k.4, p.4, 3 times and p.4, k.4, 3 times, p.4, k.1(2, 3).

58th row: P.1(2, 3), k.4, then p.4, k.4, 3 times and k.4, p.4, 3 times, k.9(10, 11).

59th row: P.2(3, 4) then k.1, p.3, 5 times, k.40(41, 42).

60th row: P.40(41, 42) then k.3, p.1, 5 times, k.2(3, 4).

61st row: As 59th row but inc. in 1st and last st.

62nd row: P.41(42, 43), then k.3, p.1, 5 times, k.3(4, 5).

63rd row: P.3(4, 5), then k.1, p.3, 5 times, k.41(42, 43).

64th row: K.41(42, 43), k.1, then p.1, k.3, 5 times, p.1, k.1(2, 3).

65th row: P.1(2, 3) then k.1, p.3, 5 times, k.1, p.1, k.41(42, 43).

66th row: As 64th row.

67th row: As 65th row but inc. 1 st. at each end of row.

68th row: K.42(43, 44), k.1, then p.1, k.3, 5 times, p.1, k.3, p.1, k.2(3, 4).

Rep. from 59th row, inc. 1 st. at each end of 73rd, 79th, 85th and 91st rows, working increased edges in patt . . . 74(76, 78) sts. Cont. in patt. and work straight until sleeve measures 46cm. Mark edges with coloured threads. Work 16 rows more in patt. Cast off loosely.

NECKBAND

Place front and back together and mark back neck along cast off edge. Sew left shoulder seam. Then with right side of back facing and 4mm needles, pick up and k.26(28, 30) sts. from back neck, 20(22, 24) sts. from left side of neck, k.10(12, 14) sts. from front spare needle and pick up and k.20(22, 24) sts. from right side of neck. Work 9 rows in k.2, p.2 rib. Cast off in the rib.

TO MAKE UP

Join right shoulder and neckband seams. Sew cast-off edges of sleeves to vertical part of armhole shaping and the rows from markers to cast off armhole edges. Sew up side and sleeve seams. Press seams carefully.

PAISLEY SLEEVELESS SLIPOVER

Materials: 4(5) 50g balls of Hayfield Grampian DK in A(Main colour), 1 ball of Hayfield Grampian DK in B and C (contrasting colours). A pair of 3mm (old size 11) and 4mm (old size 8) knitting needles.

Measurements: To fit a 81-86 (91-96) cm – 32"-34" (36"-38") bust.

Tension: 24 sts. measures about 10cm (4") over pattern.

Abbreviations: k., knit; p., purl; st.(s.), stitch(es); st.st. stocking stitch; rep., repeat; cm, centimetres; rem., remaining; inc., increase.

Size note: Follow 1st figures for 1st size and figures in brackets for 2nd size.

Metrication note: Apart from measurements above no mention of inches is made in pattern.

BACK

Using 3mm needles and A, cast on 96(100) sts. and work in k.2, p.2 rib for 9cm. Change to 4mm needles.

Next row: K.2 for 2nd size, then for both sizes, * k.7, inc. in next st. Rep. from * ending k.2 for 2nd size . . . 108(112) sts. Now with right side of work facing and working in st.st., begin at lower right hand corner of chart, reading k. rows from right to left and p. rows from left to right, beginning and ending as indicated on chart, following chart to completion working armholes and shoulders as shown. Cast off rem. sts.

FRONT

Work to match Back, but shaping neck at position marked. Cast off both sets of shoulder sts.

NECKBAND

Join left shoulder. Now using 3mm needles and A, pick up and k.94 sts. around neck edge and work in k.2, p.2 rib for 2 cm. Cast off in the rib.

ARMBANDS

Join right shoulder. Now using 3mm needles and A, pick up and k.104(108) sts. around each armhole and work in k.2, p.2 rib for 2cm. Cast off in the rib.

TO MAKE UP

Press as given on ball band. Sew up side seams, matching patterns. Darn in all loose ends.

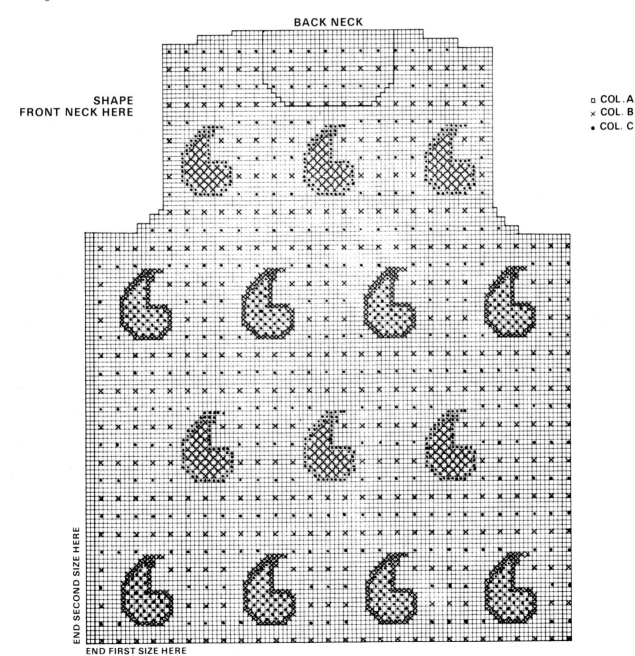

BACK NECK

SHAPE FRONT NECK HERE

□ COL. A
× COL. B
• COL. C

END SECOND SIZE HERE

END FIRST SIZE HERE

TWICE AS NICE

ARAN CARDIGAN

Materials: 3(4, 4) 50g balls of Hayfields Grampian 4 ply in Cream (49015). A pair each of 2¾mm (old No 12) and 3¼mm (Old No 10) knitting needles. Five buttons. Cable needle.

Measurements: To fit a 51(56, 61)cm – 20"(22", 24") chest. Length from shoulders 31(33, 36)cm – 12"(13", 14") Sleeve seam 21(23, 27)cm – 8¼"(9", 10½").

Tension: One complete pattern measures about 7cm (3") in width.

Abbreviations: k., knit; p., purl; st.(s), stitch(es); st.st., stocking stitch; patt., pattern; inc., increase; dec., decrease; rem., remain(ing); rep., repeat; foll., following; alt., alternate; yfwd., yarn forward; M1, make one; beg., beginning; cont., continue; tog., together; g.st., garter stitch; M., main colour; C., contrast; cm, centimetres; TW3L, slip next 2 sts. onto cable needle and leave at front of work, p.1, then k.2 from cable needle; TW3R, slip next st. on cable needle and leave at back, k.2, then p.1 from cable needle; C4B, slip next 2 sts. on cable needle, leave at Back, k. next 2 sts., then k. 2 sts. from cable needle; C4F, as C4B, but leave sts. at front of work; MB, (k.1, p.1, k.1, p.1, k.1) into next st., turn, k.5, turn p.5, turn (k.2 tog., k.1, k.2 tog.) turn, then p.3 tog.

Size note: Follow 1st figures for 1st size and figures in brackets for larger sizes.

NB: Except for measurements and tension no mention of inches is made in the patterns.

BACK.
Using 2¾mm needles cast on 70(76, 80) sts. and work in k.1, p.1 rib for 4cm.
Next row: Rib 2(5, 7), * M1, rib 6. Rep. from * 10 times more, M1 rib 2(5, 7) . . . 82(88, 92) sts.
Change to 3¼mm needles and work in patt. thus:
1st row (right side): P.2 (5, 7), * TW3L, p.1, TW3L, p.5, k.8, p.5, TW3R, p.1, TW3R * p.3, k.8, p.3. Rep. from * to *, p.2 (5, 7).
2nd and every alt. row: K. and p. sts. as they present themselves.
3rd row: P.3(6, 8) * TW3L, p.1, TW3L, p.4, C4B, C4F, p.4, TW3R, p.1, TW3R * p.4, C4B, C4F, p.4. Rep. from * to * p.3(6, 8).
5th row: P.1(4, 6) MB, p.2, * TW3L, p.1, TW3L, p.3, k.8, p.3, TW3R, p.1, TW3R * p.2, MB, p.2, k.8, p.2, MB, p.2. Rep. from * to *, p.2, MB, p.1 (4, 6).
7th row: P.4(7, 9) * TW3R, p.1, TW3R, p.3, k.8, p.3, TW3L, p.1, TW3L * p.5, k.8, p.5. Rep. from * to * p.4(7, 9).
9th row: P.3(6, 8) * TW3R, p.1, TW3R, p.4, C4F, C4B, p.4, TW3L, p1, TW3L * p.4, C4F, C4B, p.4. Rep. from * to * p.3(6, 8).
11th row: P.2(5, 7) * TW3R, p.1, TW3R, p.2, MB, p.2, k.8, p.2, MB, p.2, TW3L, p.1, TW3L *, p.3, k.8, p.3. Rep. from * to * p.2(5, 7).
12th row: As 2nd row.
These 12 rows form the patt. Cont. straight until Back measures 21(22, 24)cm ending after a wrong side row.

Shape Armholes: Cast off 3 sts. at beg. of next 2 rows, then dec. 1 st. each end of next 3 rows. Now dec. 1 st. each end of every alt. row until 62(68, 72)sts. rem. Work straight until Back measures 31(33, 36)cm ending after a wrong side row.

Shape Shoulders: Cast off 7(9, 9) sts. at beg. of next 2 rows, then 8(9, 10) sts. at beg. of next 2 rows. Cast off.

LEFT FRONT
Using 2¾mm needles cast on 35(38, 40) sts. and work in k.1, p.1 rib for 4cm.
Next row: Rib 3(5, 4), * M1, rib 7(7, 8). Rep. from * 3 times more, M1 rib 4(5, 4) . . . 40(43, 45) sts.
Change to 3¼mm needles and patt. thus:
1st row: P.2(5, 7), then rep. from * to * of 1st patt. row of Back. p.6.
2nd and alt. rows: K. and p. as sts. present themselves.
3rd row: P.3(6, 8). Rep. from * to * of 3rd patt. row of Back, p.7.
5th row: P.1(4, 6) MB, p.2. Rep. from * to * of 5th patt. row of Back, p.8.
7th row: P.4(7, 9). Rep. from * to * of 7th patt. row of Back, p.8.
9th row: P.3(6, 8). Rep. from * to * of 9th patt. row of Back, p.7.
11th row: P.2(5, 7). Rep. from * to * of 11th patt. row of Back, p.6.
12th row: As 2nd row.
These 12 rows form the patt. Cont. in patt. until work measures 10(11, 12)cm ending after a wrong side row. Now keeping continuity of patt., dec. 1 st. at end of next and every foll. 4th row until front measures as Back to armhole ending at side edge.
Shape Armhole: Keeping continuity of patt., and front decs. Cast off 3 sts. at beg. of next row, then work 1 row straight. Now dec. 1 st. at armhole edge on next 3 rows, then on next 4 alt. rows. Cont. straight at armhole edge, still dec. at front edge as before until 15(18, 19) sts. rem. Cont. straight until front measures as Back to shoulder ending at armhole edge.
Shape Shoulder: Cast off 7(9, 9) sts. at beg. of next row. Work 1 row, then cast off rem. 8(9, 10) sts.

RIGHT FRONT
Work as for Left Front reading all patt. rows and shapings in reverse, therefore 1st row will read: P.6, then rep. from * to * of 1st patt. row of Back, rib 2(5, 7).

SLEEVES
Using 2¾mm needles cast on 40(42, 44) sts. and work in k.1, p.1 rib for 3cm. Change to 3¼mm needles and patt. thus:
1st row: P.4(5, 6), then rep. from * to * of 1st patt. row of Back, p.4(5, 6).
2nd and 4th rows: K. and p. as sts. present themselves.
3rd row: Inc. in 1st st., p.4(5, 6), then rep. from * to * of 3rd patt. row of Back, p.4(5, 6), inc. in last st. Cont. in patt. as set and work to match Back, inc. 1 st. each end of 3rd and every foll. 4th row until there are 64(66, 72) sts., working inc. sts. into reversed st.st. Cont. straight until work

measures 21(23, 27)cm ending after a wrong side row.
Shape Top: Keeping continuity of patt., cast off 3 sts. at beg. of next 2 rows, then dec. 1 st. at each end of next and every alt. row until 46(46, 50) sts. rem., then each end of every row until 16 sts. rem. Cast off.
Buttonborder: Join shoulders, then using 2¾mm needles cast on 9 sts.
1st row: K.2(p.1, k.1) 3 times, k.1.
2nd row: K.1(p.1, k.1) 4 times.
Rep. last 2 rows until border, when slightly stretched, is long enough to fit up (left front for a girl, right front for a boy) to centre back neck. Cast off.
Buttonhole Border: Place pins on front edge as a guide for buttonholes, 1st pin 1cm from lower edge, 2nd pin, level with 1st front shaping and 3 more at equal distances between. Now work to match buttonborder but working buttonholes at pin positions thus: (right side) k.2, k.1, p.1, yfwd., k.2 tog., rib to end.

TO MAKE UP
Sew in sleeves, then sew up sleeve and side seams. Sew borders in position, sewing back neck edges together neatly. Sew on buttons.

FAIR ISLE SWEATERS

Materials: Of Hayfields Grampian 4 ply, 2(2, 3) 50g balls in Cream (49015) as Main shade, 1 ball 50g each of Scarlet (49012) and Hyacinth (49031) as 1st and 2nd contrasts or in Slate Blue (49038) and Sandalwood (49036) as 1st and 2nd contrasts. A pair of 2¾mm (Old No 12) and 3¼mm (Old No 10) knitting needles.

Measurements: To fit a 51(56, 61)cm – 20"(22", 24") chest. Length from top of shoulder 28(31, 33)cm – 11"(12", 13"). Sleeve seam 21(23, 27)cm – 8½"(9", 10½").

Tension: 32 sts. and 36 rows measures approx. 10cm (4").

BACK
**Using 2¾mm needles and 1st C, cast on 71(79, 85) sts. and work in k.1, p.1 rib for 4cm.
Next row: Rib 2(6, 4), * M1, rib 8(6, 7). Rep. from * 7(10, 10) times more, M1, rib 5(7, 4) . . . 81(91, 97) sts.
Change to 3¼mm needles and work in patt. thus:
1st-9th rows: Working k. rows from right to left and p. rows from left to right, beg. and ending right side rows as shown and vice versa, rep. the 6 sts. as shown on chart 13(15, 16) times across row.
10th and 11th rows: Using 1st C. p. to end.
12th-20th rows: As 7th-9th rows, but noting that chart now starts on a p. row.
21st and 22nd rows: Using 1st C. k. to end.
These 22 rows form the patt. cont. straight until Back measures about 18(20, 20)cm ending after a 10th(16th, 16th) row.
Shape Armholes: Keeping continuity of patt., cast off 4 sts. at beg. of next 2 rows, then dec. 1 st. at each end of every row until 65(71, 77) sts. rem. ** Work straight until Back measures 28(31, 33)cm. ending after a wrong side row.
Shape Shoulders: Cast off 8(9, 10) sts. at beg. of next 2 rows, then 9(10, 11) sts. at beg. of next

FAIR ISLE SWEATERS

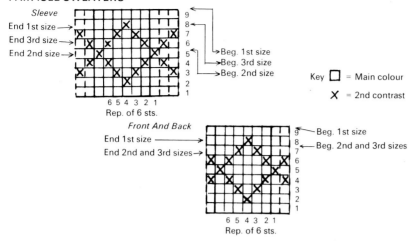

Sleeve

End 1st size →
End 3rd size →
End 2nd size →

→ Beg. 1st size
→ Beg. 3rd size
→ Beg. 2nd size

Key ☐ = Main colour

✗ = 2nd contrast

6 5 4 3 2 1
Rep. of 6 sts.

Front And Back

End 1st size ——————
End 2nd and 3rd sizes →

→ Beg. 1st size
→ Beg. 2nd and 3rd sizes

6 5 4 3 2 1
Rep. of 6 sts.

2 rows. Leave rem. 31(33, 35) sts. on a stitch holder.

FRONT
Work as for Back from ** to **. Work straight until Front measures 24(27, 29) cm ending after a wrong side row.

Divide For Neck
Next row: Patt. 24(26, 28), turn and leave rem. sts. on spare needle.
Next row: P.2 tog., patt. to end.
Cont. on these sts., dec. 1 st. at neck edge on every row until 17(19, 21) sts. rem. Work straight until Front measures as Back to shoulder, ending after a wrong side row.
Shape Shoulder: Cast off 8(9, 10) sts. at beg. of next row. Work 1 row. Cast off rem. 9(10, 11) sts. Go back to other sts., slip centre 17(19, 21) sts. on st. holder, rejoin yarn to rem. sts. and with right side facing, patt. to end.
Next row: Patt. to last 2 sts., p.2 tog. Work to match first side of neck reversing shapings.

SLEEVES
Using 2¾mm needles and 1st C. cast on 40(42, 44) sts. and work in k.1, p.1 rib for 3cm.
Next row: Rib 2(3, 4), then * M1 rib 6. Rep. from * 5 times more, M1, rib 2(3, 4) . . . 47(49, 51) sts.
Change to 3¼mm needles and work from chart for sleeves, beg. and ending as shown and repeating the 6 sts. across row 7(8, 8) times, and *beg. from the 11th(11th, 19th)* row. Inc. 1 st. each end of 3rd (3rd, 5th) row then every foll. 5th(6th, 6th) row until there are 65(67, 71) sts., working extra sts. into patt. Work straight until sleeve measures about 21(23, 27)cm ending after a 10th(16th, 16th) row of patt.
Shape Top: Keeping continuity of patt., cast off 4 sts. at beg. of next 2 rows. Now dec. 1 st. at each end of next and every foll. alt. row until 51 sts. rem. Work 1 row. Now dec. 1 st. at each end of every row until 7 sts. rem. Cast off.

Left Half Collar
Join shoulders. Then with right side of work facing, using 2¾mm needles and 1st C. slip 16(17, 18) sts. of Back on to st. holder, k. across rem. 15(16, 17) sts. inc. 3 sts. evenly across row, pick up and k. 18 sts. down left side of neck, k.8(9, 10) sts. from front inc. 3 sts. evenly across, turn – leave rem. front sts. on st. holder. Work in k.1, p.1 rib for 2cm. ending after a wrong side row.
Shape Collar
Next 2 rows: Rib to last 5 sts., turn and rib to end.
Next 2 rows: Rib to last 10 sts., turn and rib to end.
Next 2 rows: Rib to last 15 sts., turn and rib to end. Cont. in rib across all sts. until collar

measures 5cm at front edge. Cast off in rib using a 3¼mm needle.

Right Half Collar
With right side of work facing, 2¾mm needles and 1st C., k.9(10, 11) sts. from Front, inc. 2 sts. evenly across, pick up and k.18 sts. up right side, k.16(17, 18) sts. from Back, inc. 2 sts. evenly. Now work to match other half collar beg. collar shaping with wrong side of work facing.

Bow (for girl):
Using 3¼mm needles and 2nd C. cast on 56 sts. and work 6 rows in g.st. Cast off.

Bow (for boy):
Using 3¼mm needles and 2nd C. cast on 28 sts. and work 14 rows in g.st. Cast off.

TO MAKE UP
Sew in sleeves, then sew up sleeve and side seams. Join collar at Back neck edge. For the girl's sweater, form a bow and sew in position. For the boy's bow sew cast on and cast off edges together. Tightly wind yarn round centre and sew bow in position.

SKIRT, SHORTS AND SOCKS

Materials: Of Hayfields Grampian DK. **Skirt:** 3(4, 4) 50g balls in Scarlet (49, 12); **Shorts:** 3(3, 4) 50g balls in Slate Blue (49038); **Socks:** 1(1, 1) 50g ball of Hayfields Grampian 4 ply in Cream (49015) as main shade. Oddment in Scarlet/Slate Blue. A pair each of 2¾mm (Old No 12), 3¼mm (Old No 10) and 4mm (Old No 8) knitting needles. Elastic for shorts and skirt.
Measurements: These will fit a child with a 51(56, 61)cm – 20"(22", 24") chest.
Skirt: Length: 27(31, 34)cm – 10½"(12", 13½").
Shorts: Front seam, 21(22, 22)cm – 8¼"(8¾", 8¾").
Socks: Length of foot, 10(13, 15)cm – 4"(5", 6").
Tension: Using 4mm needles, 22 sts. and 30 rows to 10cm (4") (DK).
Using 3¼mm needles, 28 sts. and 36 rows to 10cm (4") (4 ply).

SKIRT

Back And Front Alike
Using 4mm needles cast on 108(114, 120) sts. and work in patt. thus:
1st row (right side): * K.1, p.5. Rep. from * to end.
2nd row: * K.4, p.2. Rep. from * to end.
3rd row: * K.3, p.3. Rep. from * to end.
4th row: * K.2, p.4. Rep. from * to end.
5th row: * K.5, p.1. Rep. from * to end.
6th row: As 4th row.
7th row: As 3rd row.
8th row: As 2nd row.
These 8 rows form the patt. Cont. in patt. until

skirt measures 24(28, 31)cm ending after a wrong side row.
Next row: * K.2 tog. k.1. Rep. from * to end . . . 72(76, 80) sts. Change to 3¼mm needles and work in k.1, p.1 rib for 9 rows. Cast off in rib.

TO MAKE UP
Join side seams. Cut elastic to fit waist, join in a ring. Work a row of herringbone stitch over elastic to form casing on wrong side of rib.

SHORTS

Back And Front Alike
Begin at top. Using 3¼mm needles cast on 56(62, 68) sts. and beg. with a k. row, work 3cm in st.st. ending after a p. row.
Next row: P. Beg. with a p. row work a further 3cm in st.st. ending with a k. row.
Next row: P.1(4, 2) * M1, p.6(6, 7). Rep. from * 8 times, M1, p.1(4, 3) . . . 66(72, 78) sts. Change to 4mm needles. Cont. in st.st. until work measures 23(24, 24)cm ending with a p. row. Divide for legs thus:
Next row: K.31(34, 37) sts., turn and leave rem. sts. on a spare needle. Cont. in st.st. on these sts. for 10cm ending with a p. row.
Next 2 rows: P. Change to 3¼mm needles and work a further 3cm in st.st. beg. with a k. row. Cast off. With right side of work facing, rejoin yarn to rem. sts., cast off centre 4 sts., k. to end. Work to match first leg.
Pockets (two Alike):
Using 4mm needles cast on 17 sts. and beg. with a k. row work in st.st. for 6cm ending with a p. row.
Next 2 rows: P. Work a further 6 rows in st.st. beg. with a k. row. Cast off.

TO MAKE UP
Join side seams. Fold waistband to wrong side, slipstitch neatly, leaving space for elastic to thread through. Cut elastic to fit waist, thread through waistband and secure. Join crutch and inside leg seams. Fold up hem at lower legs and slipstitch in position. Sew pockets onto Back of Shorts.

SOCKS
Using 2¾mm needles and 1st C. cast on 35(41, 49) sts and work in k.1, p.1 rib for 2cm. Break C. Change to 3¼mm needles and MC and beg. with a k. row work in st.st. for 3(4, 4)cm ending after a p. row. Now dec. 1 st. at each end of next and foll. 24th row, then cont. straight until leg measures 9(15, 18)cm (or length required) ending after a p. row.
Divide For Foot
Next row: K.24(28, 33), turn.
Next row: P.17(19, 21), turn. Work a further 6(8, 10)cm in st.st. on these sts. Break yarn. With right side of work facing, rejoin yarn to inside edge of 7(9, 12) sts., pick up and k.18(21, 24) sts. along right side of foot, k. across 17(19, 21) sts., inc. 3 sts. evenly across, pick up and k.18(21, 24) sts. along left side of foot, k. rem. 7(9, 12) sts. . . . 70(82, 96) sts.
Shape Foot:
1st row: K.2(4, 4), k.2 tog., k.29(33, 40) k.2 tog.) twice, k.29(33, 40) k.2 tog., k.2(4, 4).
2nd row: P.2(4, 4), p.2 tog., p.27(31, 38) then (p.2 tog.) twice, p.27(31, 38) p.2 tog., p.2(4, 4).
3rd row: K.2(4, 4), k.2 tog., k.25(29, 36) then (k.2 tog.) twice, k.25(29, 36) k.2 tog., k.2(4, 4).
4th row: P.2(4, 4), p.2 tog., p.23(27, 34) then (p.2 tog.) twice, p.23(27, 34) p.2 tog., p.2(4, 4).
5th row: K.2(4, 4) k.2 tog., k.21(25, 32) then k.2 tog.) twice, k.21(25, 32) k.2 tog., k.2(4, 4).
6th row: P.
7th row: K.
8th row: P.
Halve sts. onto 2 needles and using a 3rd needle cast off both sts. on needles together.

TO MAKE UP
Sew back and sole seams.

CREAM TOPPING

Materials: 18(20) balls of Sirdar Talisman in Cream. A 4mm (old No 8) and 3½mm (old No 9) crochet hook. A pair of 3¾ (old No 9) knitting needles. 7 buttons.

Measurements: To fit a 81-86(91-97)cm – 32"-34" (36"-38") bust. Length from top of shoulder, 54(57)cm – 21" (22½"). Sleeve seam, 43cm (17").

Tension: 17½ sts. and 14½ rows measures 10cm (4") over patt. using 4mm hook.

Abbreviations: K., knit; p., purl; st.(s), stitch(es); beg., beginning; alt., alternate; rep., repeat; patt., pattern; cm, centimetres; ch., chain; dc., double crochet; tr., treble; sp., space; lp.(s.), loop; sl.st., slip stitch; dec., decrease; dtr., double treble; inc., increase; cont., continue; rem., remain(ing).

Size note: Follow 1st figures for 1st size and figures in brackets for 2nd size.

Metrication Note: Apart from measurements above no mention of inches is made in pattern.

BACK AND FRONTS (worked in one piece to armhole):

Using 4mm hook make 171(183)ch.

Foundation Row (right side): 1 tr. in 3rd ch. from hook, 1 tr. in each st. to end – 169(181) sts. Work in patt. thus:

1st row: 1 ch., * 1 dc. in each of next 3 sts., (7 ch., miss 3 sts., 1 dc. in next st.) twice, 1 dc. in next st. Rep. from * ending 1 dc. in turning ch.

2nd row: 2 ch., miss 1st st., 1 tr. in each of next 2 sts. * (1 dtr. in each of next 3 sts. working *behind* 7-ch. lp. 1 tr. in next st.) twice, 1 tr. in each of next 4 sts. Rep. from * ending last rep. 1 tr. in each of next 2 sts.

3rd row: 1 ch., 1 dc. in each of next 4 sts., * 1 dc. in next st., working *under* 7-ch. lp, 7 ch., miss 3 sts., 1 dc. in next st. working *under* 7-ch. lp., 1 dc. in each of next 7 sts. Rep. from * ending last rep. 1 dc. in each of next 3 sts., 1 dc. in turning ch.

4th row: 2 ch., miss 1st st., * 1 tr. in each of next 4 sts., 1 dtr. in each of next 3 sts. working *behind* 7-ch. lp., 1 tr. in each of next 5 sts. Rep. from * to end.

5th row: 1 ch., * 1 dc. in each of next 6 sts., 1 dc. in next st. working *under* 7-ch. lp., 1 dc. in each of next 5 sts. Rep. from * ending 1 dc. in turning ch.

6th row: 2 ch. miss 1st st., 1 tr. in each st. to end.

7th row: 1 ch., 1 dc. in first st., 7 ch., miss 3 sts., 1 dc. in each of next 5 sts., * (7 ch., miss 3 sts., 1 dc. in next st.) twice, 1 dc. in each of next 4 sts. Rep from * ending 7 ch., miss 3 sts., 1 dc. in turning ch.

8th row: 2 ch., 1 dtr. in each of next 3 sts. working *behind* 7-ch. lp. 1 tr. in each of next 5 sts., * (1 dtr. in each of next 3 sts. as before, 1 tr. in next st.) twice, 1 tr. in each of next 4 sts. Rep. from * ending 1 dtr. in each of next 3 sts. as before, 1 tr. in last st.

9th row: 1 ch., 1 dc. in each of next 2 sts., 1 dc. in next st. working *under* 7-ch. lp., 1 dc. in each of next 7 sts., * 1 dc. in next st. working *under* 7-ch. lp., 7 ch., miss 3 sts., 1 dc. in next st. working *under* 7-ch. lp., 1 dc. in each of next 7 sts. Rep. from * ending 1 dc. in next st. working *under* 7-ch. lp. 1 dc. in next st., 1 dc. in turning ch.

10th row: 2 ch., miss 1st st., 1 tr. in each of next 10 sts., * 1 dtr. in each of next 3 sts. working *behind* 7-ch. lp., 1 tr. in each of next 9 sts. Rep. from * ending 1 tr. in last st.

11th row: 1 ch., 1 dc. in each of next 12 sts., * 1 dc. in next st. working *under* 7-ch. lp., 1 dc. in each of next 11 sts. Rep. from * ending 1 dc. in turning ch.

12th row: As 6th row. These 12 rows form the patt. Cont. straight until work measures 27cm ending with an 11th patt. row.

Divide for Armholes:

Next row: Patt. 38(41) (turning ch. equals 1 st.), turn and cont. on these sts. for Right Front. Dec. 1 st. at armhole edge on next 5 rows. Cont. straight in patt. on rem. 33(36) sts. until armhole measures 14(17)cm ending with a wrong side row.

Shape Neck:

1st row: Sl. st. over first 5 sts., patt. to end.

2nd row: Patt. to last 3 sts., 1 dc. in next st., turn.

3rd row: Sl. st. over first 2 sts., patt. to end.

4th row: As 2nd.

5th-7th row: Dec. 1 st. at neck edge. Work 3 rows on rem. 19(22) sts. ending after a wrong side row.

Shape Shoulder

1st row: Patt. to last 8(9) sts., 1 dc. in next st., turn.

2nd row: Sl. st. over first 6(7) sts., patt. to end.

3rd row: Patt. 5(6) sts., 1 dc. in next st. Fasten off. With right side of work facing, miss 8 sts., rejoin yarn to next st., 2 ch., patt. 76(82) turn. Cont. on these 77(83) sts. for Back and dec. 1 st. at each end of next 5 rows. Work straight in patt. on rem. 67(73) sts. until Back matches Right Front to beg. of shoulder shaping, thus ending after a wrong side row.

Shape Shoulders

1st row: Sl. st. over 7(8) sts., 1 dc. in next st. patt. to last 8(9) sts., 1 dc. in next st. turn.

2nd row: Sl. st. over 6(7) sts., patt. to last 6(7) sts., turn.

3rd row: Sl. st. over 6(7) sts., 1 dc. in next st., patt. to last 7(8) sts., 1 dc. in next st., turn. Fasten off. Now with right side facing, miss next 8 sts., rejoin yarn to next st., 2 ch. patt. to end – 38(41) sts. Cont. on

these sts. for Left Front and work to correspond with Right Front, reversing shapings.

SLEEVES

Make 51(57) ch. and work Foundation row as for Main part. . . 49(55) sts.

1st row (wrong side): 1 ch., 1 dc. in each of next 2(5) sts., * (7ch. miss 3 sts., 1 dc. in next st.) twice, 1 dc. in each of next 4 sts. Rep from * ending last rep. 1 dc. in each of 1(4) sts., 1 dc. in turning ch.

2nd row: 2 ch., miss 1st st., 1 tr. in each of next 2(5) sts., * (1 dtr. in each of next 3 sts. working *behind* 7-ch. lp., 1 tr. in next st.) twice, 1 tr. in each of next 4 sts. Rep from * ending last rep. 1 tr. in each of next 2(5) sts. Cont. in patt. as set and inc. 1 st. at each end of next and every following 4th row until there are 73(79) sts., taking in c. sts. into patt. Work a few rows straight until sleeve measures about 38cm ending after a 5th patt. row.

Shape Top:

1st row: Sl. st. over first 4 sts., 1 dc. in next st., patt. to last 5 sts. 1 dc. in next st., turn.

2nd row: 1 ch., miss 1st st., patt. to last st., turn.

3rd row: In patt. Rep 2nd and 3rd rows 5(6) times more, then 2nd row again . . . 51(55) sts.

Next row: Sl. st. over first 2 sts., then 1 dc. in next st., patt. to last 3 sts., 1 dc. in next st., turn.

Next row: In patt. Rep. last 2 rows 7(8) times more. Fasten off.

Armhole Frills:

Using 3½mm hook make 79(95) ch.

1st row: 1 dc. in 8th ch. from hook, * 5 ch., miss 3 ch., 1 dc. in next ch. Rep from * ending last rep. 2 ch., miss 2 ch., 1 tr. in last ch. . . . 19(23) ch. lps.

2nd row: 1 ch., 1 dc. in tr., 5 ch., miss 2 ch., * 1 dc. in dc., 3 ch., (2 tr., 1 ch., 2 tr.) in next 5-ch lp., 3 ch., 1 dc. in dc., (5 ch., 1 dc., 5 ch.) in next 5-ch. lp. Rep. from * but ending last rep 5 ch., 1 dc. in 3rd of turning ch.

3rd row: (5 ch., 1 dc., 5 ch.) in first 5-ch. lps., * 1 dc. in top of 3 ch., 3 ch., (2 tr., 1 ch., 2 tr.) in 1-ch. sp., 3 ch., 1 dc. in top of 3 ch., (5 ch., 1 dc. in next 5-ch. lps.) twice, 5 ch. Rep. from * ending last rep. 5 ch., 1 dc. in 5-ch. lp., 2 ch., 1 tr. in dc.

4th row: 1 ch., 1 dc. in tr. 5 ch., 1 dc. in next 5-ch. lp, 5 ch. * 1 dc. in top of 3-ch., 3 ch., (2 tr., 1 ch., 2 tr.) in 1-ch. sp., 3 ch., 1 dc. in top of 3-ch. (5 ch., 1 dc. in next 5-ch. lp.) 3 times, 5 ch. Rep. from * but ending last rep. 5 ch., 1 dc. in 5-ch. lp., 5 ch., 1 dc. in 3rd of turning ch.

5th row: (5 ch., 1 dc. in next 5-ch. lp.) twice, 5 ch., * 1 dc. in top of 3 ch., 3 ch., (2 tr. 1 ch., 2 tr.) in 1-ch sp., 3 ch., 1 dc. in top of 3-ch. (5 ch., 1 dc. in next 5-ch. lp) 4 times, 5 ch. Rep. from * ending last rep. (5 ch., 1 dc. in next 5-ch. lp.) twice, 2 ch., 1 tr. in dc.

6th row: 1 ch., 1 dc. in tr. (5 ch., 1 dc. in next 5-ch. lp.) twice, 5 ch., * 1 dc. in top of 3 ch., 3 ch. (2 tr., 1 ch., 2 tr.) in 1-ch. sp., 3 ch., 1 dc. in top of 3 ch. (5 ch., 1 dc. in next 5-ch. lp.) 5 times. Rep. from * ending last rep (5 ch., 1 dc. in next 5-ch lp.) twice, 5 ch., 1 dc. in 3rd of turning ch. Fasten off.

NECK FRILL

Make 78(86) ch. and work 1st to 4th rows as for Armhole Frill. Fasten off.

TO MAKE UP

Do not press.

Welt: With right side of work facing and using 3¾mm needles pick up and k. 169(181) sts. along lower edge of main part and work 5cm in k.1, p.1 rib, with rows on wrong side beginning and ending with a p. st. Cast off in the rib. Join shoulder seams. Tack Collar Frill in place beg. and ending at centre front.

Front and Neck Borders: Using 3½mm hook and with right side of work facing, beg. at lower edge of welt and work in dc. up right front inc. 2 sts. at corner st., work in dc. round neck, working through collar frill and main part, then work down left front to lower edge, inc. 2 sts. at corner st. as before.

2nd row: In dc., dec. 2 sts. at back neck, and with the addition of 7 buttonholes on right front, 1st. to come 2cm below top of neck border, last to come 2cm above lower edge and remainder spaced evenly between, working buttonholes thus: 2 ch., miss 2 sts., 1 dc. in next st. (worked over each buttonhole position). In next row work 2 dc into each 2-ch. sp. and inc. 2 sts. at each corner as before. Fasten off.

CUFFS With right side facing and using 3¾mm needles pick up and k. 43(47) sts. along lower edge of each sleeve and work as for Welt. Join sleeve seams. Tack armhole frill round armholes. Sew in sleeves, sewing through all three thicknesses and gathering sleeve head to fit. Press seams lightly. Sew on buttons.

SHAPELY CARDIGAN

Materials: 8 50g balls of Hayfield Gaucho in main colour (grey), 6 balls in purple, 5 balls in turquoise, 3 balls each in black and gold. 1 pair each of 3¾mm (Old No 9) and 5mm (Old No 6) knitting needles, 7 buttons.

Measurements: To fit 86-91 (97-102)cm 32"-34" (36"-38") bust. Length 63cm (24¾"). Sleeve Seam 48cm (18¼").

Tension: 18 sts. and 20 rows to 10cm (4") over patt on 5mm needles.

Abbreviations: alt., alternate; beg., beginning; cont., continue; dec., decrease; foll., following; inc., increase; k., knit; p., purl; patt., pattern; rem., remain; rep., repeat; st.(s.) stitch(es); st. st., stocking stitch; A, grey; B, black; C, gold; D, purple; E, turquoise.

BACK

With 5mm needles and B, cast on 81 sts. and start at left side seam, working in st.st. as folls:

1st row: K.1 A (edge st.), k. the 44 sts. of chart, then the first 36 sts. again.

2nd row: Reading the chart from left to right p. from 36th st. to 1st st. then from 44th to 1st sts. and edge st. Cont. in patt from chart as set, rep. the 24 rows throughout, *at the same time* inc. one st. at beg. of 4th(6th) and every foll. 4th row until there are 89 sts., working the extra sts. into patt., then work 2(4) rows. 34(38) rows from beg.**
Place a marker at shaped edge of last row to denote beg. of neck.
Work 26(30) rows straight, then place another marker to denote end of neck.
Work 2(4) rows. Dec one st. at end of next and every foll. 4th row until 81 sts. rem., then work 3(5) rows. 94(106) rows from beg. Cast off.

RIGHT FRONT

Work as given for Back to **, then k. 1 row.

Shape Neck

Cast off 4 sts. at beg. of next and foll. 2 alt. rows, 2 sts. at beg. of foll. 2 alt. rows, then dec. one st. at beg. of foll. alt. row. Work 2(4) rows, then cast off rem. 72 sts.

LEFT FRONT

With 5mm needles and B, cast on 81 sts.

and start at side seam. Turn chart upside down and work pattern in reverse as foll.:

1st row: Working 22nd row of chart, k. from 36th st. to 1st st, from 44th to 1st sts., then k. edge st.

2nd row: Working 21st row of chart, p. edge st., p. 1st to 44th sts., then 1st to 36th sts. Cont. in patt. as set to match Right Front, reversing all shaping.

SLEEVES (Both alike)

With 5mm needles and B, cast on 57 sts. and work sleeve from side seam to side seam.

1st row: K. edge st., k. 1st to 44th sts., then 1st to 12th sts.

2nd row: P. 12th to 1st sts., 44th to 1st sts., then p. edge st. Work 8 more rows from chart as set.

11th row: K. 12B, 22C, 23B.

12th row: P. 23B, 22C, 12B.

Work 13th to 22nd rows from chart as already set.

23rd row: K. 12C, 22B, 23C.

24th row: P. 23C, 22B, 12C.

Rep these 24 rows until 84(84) rows have been worked in all. Cast off.

CUFFS

With 3¾mm needles and D, cast on 47(53)sts.

1st row: K. 1, * p.1, k.1, rep. from * to end.

2nd row: P.1, * k.1, p.1, rep. from * to end. Rep. these 2 rows throughout, work 4 more rows in D, 1 row A, 2 rows C, 1 row A, 6 rows E, 1 row A, 2 rows B, 1 row A, then rep. the first 16 rows again.
Cast off in rib.

WELT AND FRONT BANDS

With 3¾mm needles and D, cast on 171(181) sts. and work 36 rows in rib as on cuffs, at the same time making buttonholes on 8th and 28th rows as folls: Rib to last 8 sts., cast off 4, rib 4. On next row cast on 4 sts. over the 4 cast off.

37th row: Rib 12, cast off 147(157), rib rem. 12 sts. Cont. in rib in stripe patt. on last 12 sts. until 130 rows in all have been worked from beg. Break off yarn and leave sts. on holder. Return to the rem. 12 sts. and work to match, making buttonholes as before on every 20th row. Do not break off yarn.

COLLAR

Join shoulder seams. With 3¾mm needles and D and right side facing rib the 12 sts. of right front band, pick up and k.18(19) sts. up right front neck, 27(31) sts. across back neck, 18(19) sts. down left front neck, then rib the 12 sts. of left front band. 87(93)sts. Cont. in rib, work 3 rows.

Next row: Rib 12, * (k.1, p.1, k.1) into next st., rib 5, rep. from * to last 15 sts., (k.1, p.1, k.1) into next st., rib 14. 109(117) sts. Cont. in rib in stripe patt. as before, work 31 rows, thus ending with 16th patt. row. Cast off in rib.

TO MAKE UP

Press work according to instructions on ball band. Sew in sleeves. Join side and sleeve seams. Join seam of cuffs and sew to sleeves, gathering sleeves to fit. Sew on welt and front bands. Press all seams. Sew on buttons.

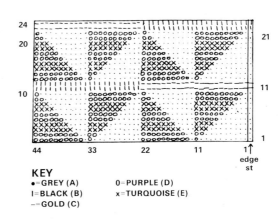

KEY
- ● = GREY (A)
- I = BLACK (B)
- — = GOLD (C)
- 0 = PURPLE (D)
- x = TURQUOISE (E)

LACY KNIT TOP

Materials: 10(11) 50g balls Pingouin Fil d'Ecosse No 5 cotton. A pair of 3¾mm (old No 9) and 2¾mm (old No 12) knitting needles.
Measurements: To fit an 81cm-86cm (91-96)cm – 32"-34" (36"-38") bust.
Tension: 34 sts. measures 10cm (4") over eyelet patt. using 2¾mm needles.

Abbreviations: K., knit; p., purl; st.(s.), stitch(es); cont., continue; patt., pattern; rem., remain(ing); beg., beginning; yo., yarn over; sl., slip; tog., together; psso., pass slip st. over; p2sso., pass the 2 slip sts. over; tbl., through back of loop; mb., make bobble (k.1, yo., k.1, yo., k.1) into same st., turn, p.5, turn, k.5, turn, p.5, turn, k.5, turn, p.2 tog., p.1, p.2 tog., turn, sl.l, k.2 tog., psso.; rep., repeat. Cluster=slip the given number of sts. with yarn to back, pass yarn to front, slip the same sts. back to left-hand needle, pass yarn to back, slip the same sts. again with yarn to back, thus winding yarn round the slip sts.

Size note: Where 2 figures are given follow 1st figures for 1st size and figures in brackets for 2nd size.
Metrication note: Apart from measurements above, no reference to inches is made in pattern.
BACK
Using 3¾mm needles cast on 177(199) sts. and work border thus:
**1st row: (right side facing): k.1, * yo. (k.1 tbl., p.3) 5 times, k.1 tbl., yo., k.1. Rep. from * to end.

2nd row: P.3, * (k.3, p.1) 4 times, k.3, p.5. Rep. from * ending p.3 instead of p.5.
3rd row: K.1, * yo., k.1 tbl., yo. (k.1 tbl., p.3) 5 times, (k.1 tbl., yo.) twice, k.1. Rep. from * to end.
4th row: P.5, * (k.3, p.1) 4 times, k.3, p.9. Rep. from * ending p.5 instead of p.9.
5th row: K.1, * yo., k.1 tbl., yo., sl.1, k.1, psso., yo., (k.1 tbl., p.2 tog., p.1) 5 times, k.1 tbl., yo., k.2 tog., yo., k.1 tbl., yo., k.1. Rep. from * to end.
6th row: P.7, * (k.2, p.1) 4 times, k.2, p.13. Rep. from * ending p.7 instead of p.13.
7th row: K.1, * k.1 tbl., (yo., sl.1, k.1, psso.) twice, yo., (k.1 tbl., p.2) 5 times, k.1 tbl., yo., (k.2 tog., yo.) twice, k.1 tbl., k.1. Rep. from * to end.
8th row: P.8, * (k.2, p.1) 4 times, k.2, p.15. Rep. from * ending p.8 instead of p.15.
9th row: K.2, * (yo. k.2 tog.) twice, yo., k.1 tbl., yo., (k.1 tbl., p.2 tog.) 5 times, (k.1 tbl., yo.) twice, (sl.1, k.1, psso., yo.) twice, k.3. Rep. from * ending k.2 instead of k.3.
10th row: P.10, * (k.1, p.1) 4 times, k.1, p.19. Rep. from * ending p.10 instead of p.19.
11th row: Sl.1, k.1, psso., * (yo., k.2 tog.) 3 times, k.1 tbl., yo., (k.1 tbl., p.1) 5 times, k.1 tbl., yo., k.1 tbl., (sl.1, k.1, psso., yo.) 3 times, sl.2, k.1, p.2sso. Rep. from * ending last rep. k.2 tog. instead of sl.2, k.1, p.2sso.
12th row: As 10th row.
13th row: K.1, * (k.2 tog., yo.) twice, k.2 tog., k.1, k.1 tbl., yo., (sl.1, k.1, psso.) twice, sl.1, k.2 tog., psso., (k.2 tog.) twice, yo., k.1 tbl., k.1, sl.1, k.1, psso., (yo., sl.1, k.1., psso.) twice, k.1. Rep. from * to end.
14th row: Cluster 2, * p.7, cluster 5, p.7, cluster 3. Rep. from * ending with cluster 2 instead of 3. Change to 2¾mm needles and cont. thus:
Next row: K.11*, mb., k.21. Rep. from * ending k.11 instead of k.21.
Next row: P.
Next row: K. **
Next row: P.9, * p.2 tog., p.1, p.2 tog., p.17. Rep. from * ending p.9 instead of p.17 ... 161(181) sts. Cont. in eyelet patt. as follows:
1st row (right side facing): K.
2nd row: P.
3rd row: * K.6, yo., k.2 tog. Rep. from * to last st., k.1 (k.5).
4th row: P.
5th row: K.
6th row: P.
7th row: K.2, * yo., k.2 tog., k.6. Rep. from * to last 7(3) sts., yo., k.2 tog., k.5 (1).
8th row: P. Rep. rows 1-8 inclusive 19 times more.
Shape for Sleeves:
Keeping continuity of patt. cast on 5 sts. at

beg. of next 2 rows, 6 sts. at beg. of next 2 rows and 10 sts. at beg. of next 2 rows. 203(223) sts. *** Cont. in patt. for 70 more rows.
Shape Shoulders:
Cast off 16(18) sts. at beg. of next 2 rows, 18(20) sts. at beg. of next 2 rows and 22(24) sts. at beg. of next 2 rows. Cast off rem. sts.
FRONT
Work exactly as for Back to ***.
Cont. thus: Work 52 rows in patt.
Shape Neck
Next row: Patt. 81(87) sts., and leave on spare needle, cast off next 41(49) sts., patt. to end.
Next row (wrong side facing): P.
Next row: Cast off 8 sts., k. to end.
Next row: P.
Next row: Cast off 6 sts., cont. in patt. to end.
Next row: P.
Next row: Cast off 4 sts., k. to end.
Next row: P. to last 2 sts., p.2 tog.
Next row: Cast off 3 sts., in patt. to end.
Next row: P. to last 2 sts., p.2 tog.
Next row: K.2 tog., k. to end.
Next row: P. to last 2 sts., p.2 tog. Keeping continuity of patt. work 7 work straight.
Shape Shoulder:
Next row: Cast off 16(18) sts., p. to end.
Next row: In patt. to end.
Next row: Cast off 18(20) sts., p. to end.
Next row: K. Cast off rem. 22(24) sts. Go back to other sts., rejoin yarn and with wrong side of work facing, work thus:
Next row: Cast off 8 sts., p. to end.
Next row: K.
Next row: Cast off 6 sts., p. to end.
Next row: In patt.
Next row: Cast off 4 sts., p. to end.
Next row: K. to last 2 sts., k.2 tog.
Next row: Cast off 3 sts., p. to end.
Next row: Work in patt. to last 2 sts., k.2 tog.
Next row: P.2 tog., p. to end.
Next row: K. to last 2 sts., k.2 tog. Work 7 rows straight, then shape shoulder to match other side.

SLEEVE BORDERS (2 required)
Using 3¾mm needles cast on 111 sts. for each size and work from ** to ** as for Back. Cast off.

NECKBAND
Join right shoulder and mark neck point on other side. Then with right side of work facing, and 2¾mm needles pick up and k.202(222) sts. around neck and work in k.2 p.2 rib for 2cm. Cast off in the rib.

TO MAKE UP
Join left shoulder and neckband. Sew on sleeve borders, then sew up side seams.

SQUARE SET

Materials: 16(17, 17)g balls Sirdar Talisman in Main. 3(3, 3)g balls Sirdar Talisman in Contrast. A pair of 3¼mm (Old No 10) and 4mm (Old No 8) knitting needles. A medium size crochet hook.

Measurements: To fit a 91(96, 102)cm – 36″(38″, 40″) bust. Length from centre back neck, 81cm (32″).

Tension: 12 sts measure 5cm (2″) over st. st. using 4mm (Old No 8) needles.

Abbreviations: k., knit; p., purl; st. (s.), stitch(es); st.st., stocking stitch; rep., repeat; alt., alternate; beg., beginning; tog., together; y.r.n., yarn round needle; cont., continue; dec., decrease; patt., pattern; inc., increase; rem., remain(ing); M, main; C, contrast.

Size note: Where 3 figures are given follow 1st figures for 1st size, 2nd figures for 2nd size and 3rd figures for 3rd size.

Metrication note: Except for above no mention of inches is made in pattern.

BACK
Using 3¼mm needles and M cast on 117(123, 129) sts. and work in k.1, p.1 rib, beg. and ending right side rows with a k. st. and wrong side rows with a p. st., and work for 9cm. Change to 4mm needles. Work in patt. thus:

1st row: K.38(40, 42), p.1, k.39(41, 43), p.l, k.38(40, 42).

2nd row: P.38(40, 42), k.1, p.39(41, 43), k.1, p.38(40,42). Rep. last 2 rows 4 times more.

11th row: Join in C and work as 1st row using C.

12th row: Using C. As 2nd row. Using M rep. 1st and 2nd rows 7 times.

27th row: K.38(40, 42), p.1, k.17(18, 19), p.5, k.17(18, 19), p.1, k.38(40, 42).

28th row: P.38(40, 42), k.1, p.17(18, 19), k.5, p.17(18, 19), k.1, p.38(40, 42). Rep. last 2 rows once.

31st row: K.38(40, 42), p.1, k.17(18, 19), p.2, y.r.n., p.2 tog., p.1, k.17(18, 19), p.1, k.38(40, 42).

32nd-34th rows: Rep. 28th, 27th and 28th rows once.

35th-48th rows: Rep. 1st and 2nd rows 7 times.

49th-50th rows: Using C rep. 1st and 2nd rows.

51st-64th rows: Rep. 1st and 2nd rows 7 times.

65th row: K.16(17, 18), p.5, k.17(18, 19), p.1, k.39(41, 43), p.1, k.17(18, 19), p.5, k.16(17, 18).

66th row: P.16(17, 18), k.5, p.17(18, 19), k.1, p.39(41, 43), k.1, p.17(18, 19), k.5, p.16(17, 18). Rep last 2 rows once more.

69th row: K.16(17, 18), p.2, y.r.n., p.2 tog., p.1, k.17(18, 19), p.1, k.39(41, 43), p.1, k.17(18, 19), p.2, y.r.n., p.2 tog, p.1, k.16(17, 18).

70th row: As 66th row.

71st row: As 65th row.

72nd row: As 66th row. Rep. the 1st and 2nd rows 7 times more. Rep. from 11th row until work measures 80cm from beg. ending after a wrong side row.

Shape Shoulders:
Cast off 20(21, 22) sts. at beg. of next 2 rows then 21(22, 23) sts. at beg. of next 2 rows. Cast off rem. sts.

FRONT
Work as for Back until the 26th row has been worked. Now work from row 65 to 72 inclusive. Cont. in patt. working small squares in every alt. large square until work measures 74cm from beg. ending after a wrong side row.

Shape Neck:
Next row: Patt. 49(51, 53), cast off 19(21, 23) sts., patt. to end. Cont. on last set of sts., k.2 tog. at neck edge on every row until 41(43, 45) sts. rem. Cont. straight until front measures as Back ending at armhole edge.

Shape Shoulder:
Cast off 20(21, 22) sts. at beg. of next row Work 1 row, then cast off rem. 21(22, 23) sts. Go back to rem. sts., rejoin yarn and work to match first side.

SLEEVES
Read sleeve instructions through, before beginning work.
Using 3¼mm needles and M cast on 59(61, 63) sts. and work in k.1, p.1 rib for 5cm. Change to 4mm needles and beg. patt. thus:

1st row: K.9, p.1, k.39(41, 43), p.1, k.9.

2nd row: P.9, k.1, p.39(41, 43), k.1, p.9. Rep. 1st and 2nd rows 4 times more then using C, work 2 rows. Cont. in patt. making a small square as before in the centre of alt. large squares, *but at the same time*, inc. 1 st. at each end of the 5th row *after welt*, and every foll. 6th row until there are 105(107, 109) sts., allowing for inc. sts. at beg. and end of rows. Cont. straight until sleeve measures 53cm. Cast off.

COLLAR
Using 3¼mm and M cast on 133(137, 141) sts. and work in k.1, p.1 rib for 2.5cm. Change to 4mm needles and cont. in rib until collar measures 13cm. Cast off in the rib.

TO MAKE UP
Press as instructions on ball band. Using the crochet hook and C, work a chain up each p. st. from above welt to shoulder. Join shoulders. Mark depth of armholes from shoulder seams. Sew in sleeves then join sleeve and side seams. Sew on collar. Turn back cuffs.

SCARF
Using C and 4mm needles cast on 28 sts. and work thus:

1st row: K.9, p.1, k.8, p.1, k.9.

2nd row: K.2, p.7, k.1, p.8, k.1, p.7, k.2. Rep. these 2 rows 5 times more. Change to M and work 2 rows. Change to C* work 18 rows C, then 2 rows M. Rep. from* 17 times more. Work 12 rows C and cast off. Press as given on ball band. Using M and crochet hook, work a chain up the p. ridges. Turn the garter st. borders to wrong side and slip-stitch down neatly. Using C work a knotted fringe along short edges of scarf.

MUSTARD 'N' DRESS

Materials: 22 50g balls of Emu Finlandia in Main. 4 50g balls of Emu Finlandia in Contrast. A pair of 4½mm (Old No 7) and 5½mm (Old No 5) knitting needles. A cable needle.
Measurements: To fit a 91-96cm (36"-38") bust.
Tension: 15 sts. measures just under 10cm (4") over main patt.

Abbreviations: K., knit; p., purl; st.(s.), stitch(es); sl., slip; cont., continue; patt., pattern; rem., remain(ing); rep., repeat; st.st., stocking stitch; C6B, slip 3 sts. on to cable needle and leave at back of work, k. next 3 sts., then k.3 sts. from cable needle.; C6F, As C6B but leave sts. on cable needle at front; twist 3L., drop sl.st. to front of work, k. next 2 sts., then pick up dropped st. and knit it; twist 3R – sl. next 2 sts. to right hand needle, drop sl.st. to front of work, sl. the 2 sts. back to left hand needle K the 2sts., then pick up dropped st. and k. it; pw., purlwise; yf., yarn to front of work; yb., yarn to back of work; inc., increase; dec., decrease; psso., pass slip stitch over; tog., together; M, main; C, contrast.

Metrication Note: Except for above no mention of inches is made in pattern.
BACK
Using 4½mm needles and M, cast on 92 sts. and work thus:
1st row: (wrong side) (K.2, p.3) 9 times, k.2, (p.3, k.2) 9 times.
2nd row: (P.2, k.2, sl.1 pw., yf.) 9 times, p.2, (yb. sl.1 pw., k.2, p.2) 9 times.
3rd row: (K.2, p.2, keep yarn in front, sl.1 pw., yb.,)9 times, k.2, (yf., sl.1 pw., p.2, k.2) 9 times.
4th row: (P.2, twist 3R) 9 times, p.2, (twist 3L, p.2) 9 times. Rep. these 4 rows 3 times more. Change to 5½mm needles.
Next row: (wrong side) P.45, inc. in next st., p. to end . . . 93 sts. Join on C and cont. in main patt. thus:
1st row: With C. K.1, * yf., sl.1 pw., yb., sl.2 Rep. from * ending yf., sl.1 pw., k.1.
2nd row: P.1, * yb., sl.1 pw., yf., sl.2. Rep. from * ending yb., sl.1 pw., p.1.
3rd–6th rows: In st.st. using M.
These 6 rows form the patt. Rep. them 34 times more (or length required to arm-holes) then work 1st and 2nd rows once more.
Shape Armholes: Keeping continuity of patt., cast off 4 sts. at beg. of next 2 rows ***. Now dec. 1 st. each end of next and every st.st. row (thus working straight on the 2 patt. rows) until 23 sts. rem. Cont. straight until 45 complete patts. from beg. have been worked. Leave sts. on st. holder.

FRONT
Work as for Back to ***. Now dec. 1 st. each end of every st.st. row until 29 sts. rem. and ending after a wrong side row.
Shape Neck:
Next row: K.2 tog., k.5 and leave these sts. on spare needle, cast off next 15 sts., k.5 – including st. already on right hand needle from cast-off, k.2 tog.
Next row: P.2 tog., p.4.
Next row: K.3, k.2 tog.
Next row: P.2, p.2 tog.   **Next row:** K.3.
Next row: P.1, p.2 tog.   **Next row:** K.2.
Next row: P.2, and cast off.
With wrong side facing, rejoin yarn and work to match other side.
SLEEVES
Using 4½mm needles and M cast on 42 sts. and work 13 rows of welt rib as for back welt, but repeating sts. in brackets 4 times instead of 9.
14th row: K.1, * k.3, inc. in next st. Rep. from * to last st., k.1. (52 sts.)
Next row: P. to end.
Change to 5½mm needles. Now beg. with a k. row cont. in st.st. inc. 1 st. each end of next and every 4th row following until there are 72 sts. Work 3 rows in st.st. beg. with a p. row. Now work in patt. thus:
1st row: Inc. in 1 st. k.26, (p.2, k.6) twice, p.2, k.26, inc. in last st.
2nd row: P.28, (k.2, p.6) twice, k.2, p.28.
3rd row: K.28, (p.2, k.6) twice, p.2, k.28.
4th row: As 2nd row.
5th row: Inc. in 1 st., k.27, p.2, C6B, p.2, C6F, p.2, k.27, inc. in last st. Cont. thus inc. 1 st. each end of every 4th row, *at the same time* working cable patt. panel as before and cabling on every 6th row until there are 86 sts. (25th row completed).
26th row: P.34, (k.2, p.6) twice, k.2, p.34.
Shape Top: Keeping continuity of centre 18 patt. sts. throughout, cont. thus.
27th row: Cast off 4 sts., p.2 – including st. on right hand needle from casting off, k.6, p.2, k.20, patt. 18, k.20, p.2, k.6, p.2, k.4.
28th row: Cast off 4 sts., k.2 – including st. on right hand needle from casting off., p.6, k.2, p.20, patt. 18, p.20, k.2, p.6, k.2.
29th row: P.2, k.6, p.2, sl.1, k.1, psso., k.18, patt.18, k.18, k.2 tog., p.2, k.6, p.2.
30th row: K.2, p.6, k.2, p.19, patt.18, p.19, k.2, p.6, k.2.
31st row: P.2, k.6, p.2, sl.1, k.1, psso., k.17, patt.18, k.17, k.2 tog., p.2, k.6, p.2.
32nd row: K.2, p.6, k.2, p.18, patt.18, p.18, k.2, p.6, k.2.
33rd row: P.2, k.6, p.2, sl.1, k.1, psso., k.16, patt.18, k.16, k.2 tog., p.2, k.6, p.2.
34th row: K.2, p.6, k.2, p.17, patt.18, p.17, k.2, p.6, k.2.
35th row: P.2, C6B, p.2, sl.1, k.1, psso.,

k.15, patt.18, k.15, k.2 tog., p.2, C6F, p.2. Cont. thus keeping continuity of centre panel as before and dec. 1 st. each end, inside the 10 border sts., and cabling as given (see 35th row) on every 6th row until 40 sts. rem., thus ending after a cable row. Cont. thus:
66th row: (wrong side) K.2, p.6, k.2, p.1, patt.18, p.1, k.2, p.6, k.2.
67th row: P.2, k.6, p.2, k.1, patt.18, k.1, p.2, k.6, p.2.
Rep. last 2 rows once more, then 66th row again.
71st row: P.2, C6B, p.2, k.1, patt.18, k.1, p.2, C6F, p.2.
Rep. 66th–71st rows once more, then 66th row again. Sl. sts. on to st. holder.
NECKBAND
Sew in sleeves, leaving left back raglan open. Now using 4½mm needles and M and with right side of work facing, k. across 40 sts. from 1st sleeve, pick up and k.27 sts. around front neck, k.40 sts. from 2nd sleeve, then k. across back 23 sts . . . 130 sts.
With **right side of collar** facing (collar turns back) cont. thus:
1st row: * p.2, yb., sl.1 pw., k.2. Rep. from * to end.
2nd row: * P.2, sl.1 pw., yb., k.2. Rep. from * to end.
3rd row: * P.2, twist 3L. Rep. from * to end.
4th row: * P.3, k.2. Rep. from * to end.
Rep. these 4 rows until collar measures 20cm. Cast off in the rib.
TO MAKE UP.
Press as given on ball band. Sew up raglan and collar seam, allowing seam for turn back, ie half will be sewn on wrong side and half on right side. Sew up sleeve and side seams. Make tassels and sew on to sleeves as shown in photograph.

YARN STOCKISTS

IN GREAT BRITAIN

Hayfield Textiles Ltd

Hayfield Mills
Glusburn
Keighley
West Yorkshire
BD20 8QP
Tel: Cross Hills 33333

Sirdar Ltd

Flanshaw Lane
Alverthorpe
Wakefield
West Yorkshire
WF2 9ND
Tel: Wakefield 371501

Patricia Roberts Knitting Shop
60 Kinnerton Street
London SW1X 8ES
Tel: 01-602 4913

Pingouin

French Wools Ltd
7-11 Lexington Street
London W1R 4BU
Tel: 01-439 8891

Phildar UK Ltd

4 Gambrel Road
Westgate Industrial Estate
Northampton
NN5 5NF
Tel: Northampton 583111

Robin Wools Ltd

Robin Mills
Idle
Bradford
West Yorkshire
BD10 9TE
Tel: Bradford 612561

3 Suisses

Marlborough House
38 Welford Road
Leicester
LE2 7AA
Tel: Leicester 28173

Twilleys

H G Twilley Ltd
Roman Mill
Little Casterton Road
Stamford
Lincolnshire
PE9 1BG
Tel: Stamford 52661

Patons & Baldwins Ltd

Kilncraigs Mill
Alloa
Clackmannanshire
Scotland
FK10 1EG
Tel: Alloa 723431

Emu Wools

Customer Service Dept
Leeds Road
Greengates
Bradford
West Yorkshire
BD10 9TE
Tel: Bradford 612561

IN AUSTRALIA AND SOUTH AFRICA

Patons & Baldwins (including Jaeger)

Coats Patons (Australia) Ltd
PO Box 110
Ferntree Gully Road
Mount Waverley
Victoria
Australia

Patons & Baldwins South Africa Pty Ltd
PO Box 33
Randfontein 1760
Transvaal
South Africa

Emu and Robin

The Needlewoman
Karingal
Grove
Huon
Hobart 7106
Tasmania

E Brasch & Son
57 La Rochelle Road
Trojan
Johannesburg
South Africa

Twilleys

Panda Yarns (International) Pty
17-27 Brunswick Road
East Brunswick
Victoria 3057
Australia

F W Nyman & Co Ltd
PO Box 292
Durban 4000
South Africa

Chester Mortonson
PO Box 11179,
Johannesburg 2000
South Africa

Patricia Roberts

Colin Joyce
Myladys
238 Flinders Lane
Victoria
Australia

None in SA

Hayfield

Panda Yarns (International) Pty Ltd
(for address see under Twilleys)

A & H Agencies
392 Commissioner Street
Fairview
Johannesburg 2094
South Africa

Sirdar

Coats Patons (Australia) Pty Ltd
(for address see under Patons &
Baldwins)

Sirdar Wool (Pty) Ltd
PO Box 33
Randfontein 1760
South Africa

3 Suisses

Filature de L'Espierres
7760 Dottignies
Belgium
(Will supply by mail order worldwide)

Pingouin

R Mestdagh
Pingouin Export
BP 9110
59061
Rubaix
Sedex 1
France
(Write to above address for stockists in
Australia)

Pingouin Wools
Promatex
PO Box 12012
Jacobs 4026
Natal
South Africa

ACKNOWLEDGEMENTS

Ruffle Blouse
Photograph by Chris Dawes

Big Softie
Designed by Eva Hazra.
Photographed by Di Lewis

Star-Spangled Jacket
Photographed by Di Lewis

Jack of Hearts Pullover
Designed by Alan Dart

Mohair Kimono and Slipover
Designed by Debbie Hudson

Chevron Sweater
Designed by Sue Griffin

Twice as Nice
Designed by Tina Clark.
Photographed by Di Lewis

Tip-Top Tunic
Photographed by Phil Babb

Mohair Jacket
Designed by Tina Clark.
Photographed by Chris Dawes

Half Sleeve Roll Neck
Photographed by Peter Waldman

Bobble Cardigan
Designed by Patricia Roberts.
Photographed by Rob Lee

Wrap-Over Cardigan
Photographed by Peter Waldman

Fair Isle Twin Set
Photographed by Tom Leighton

Argyle Slip-Over
Photographed by Di Lewis

Pastel Plaid Cardigan
Photographed by Colin Thomas

Paisley Pullover in Mohair
Photographed by Di Lewis

Cotton Cable Cardigan
Photographed by Matt White

Party Piece
Designed by Debbie Hudson
Photographed by Murray Irving

Frilled Alpaca Sweater
Designed by Julia Pines

Gilt-Edged Cardigan
Designed by Ross and Cross

Paisley Skirt and Top
Designed by Val Moon

Cream Topping
Photographed by Di Lewis

Deftly Textured Sweater
Designed by Val Moon.
Photographed by Di Lewis

Aztec Jacket
Photographed by Di Lewis

Paisley Sleeveless Slipover
Designed by Val Moon.
Photographed by Roger Eaton

Shapely Cardigan
Designed by Mary Norden.
Photographed by Di Lewis

Lacy Knit Top
Photographed by Roger Eaton

Square Set
Photographed by Di Lewis

Mustard 'N' Dress
Designed by Val Moon.
Photographed by Di Lewis